GREAT
DADS

Robert Hamrin

GREAT DADS

Building
loving
lasting
relationships
with your
kids

Creating Teachable Moments
faithparenting.com

Faith Parenting is an imprint of
Cook Communications Ministries, Colorado Springs, Colorado 80918
Cook Communications, Paris, Ontario
Kingsway Communications, Eastbourne, England

GREAT DADS
© 2002 by Robert D. Hamrin

First Printing, 1993
Printed in the United States of America

1 2 3 4 5 6 7 8 9 10 Printing/Year 06 05 04 03 02

Senior Editor: Janet Lee
Cover Design: Granite Design
Interior Design: Granite Design

Unless otherwise noted, the Bible version used in this publication is THE NEW KING
JAMES VERSION. Copyright © 1979, 1980, 1982, Thomas Nelson, Inc., Publishers.

Scripture noted NIV is taken from the HOLY BIBLE, NEW INTERNATIONAL VER-
SION®. Copyright © 1973, 1978, 1984 by International Bible Society. Used by permission of Zondervan Publishing House. All rights reserved.

Printed in the United States of America.

Hamrin, Robert D.
    [Straight from a dad's heart]
    Great dads/ by Robert D. Hamrin.
        p. cm.
Originally published: Straight from a dad's heart. Nashville : T.
Nelson, c1993.
    ISBN 0-7814-3818-7
    1. Fatherhood--United States. 2. Father and child--United States. I.
Title.
    HQ756 .H356 2002
    306.874'2--dc21   2002000569

CONTENTS

FOREWORD

NO BOOK on the family is more needed today than Bob Hamrin's *Great Dads*—and perhaps no one is better qualified to write it. Bob has applied both his brilliant mind and his deep commitment to Christ to this challenging subject.

It is full of practical advice, true stories that illustrate the various situations, and tremendous wisdom.

Even though I am by now a great-grandfather, I realize as long as I have a son, no matter how old he is, I am still his father. For that reason this book has no age limit. I can learn much from it. So can you. In today's world this is of paramount importance.

God bless us all as we read and apply this God-given book.

Billy Graham

To the memory of my dad, Charles,
Who showed me the joy of fathering for over
forty-five years.

To my children Eric, Kira, and Krista,
Who bring joy into my life each
and every day.

A Tribute to My Dad

IT IS sadly ironic that during the course of my writing this book, my dad passed from life to death. This reality hit home to me most as I was sitting down to write the conclusion less than a month after he passed away. He is no longer with me as he was when I started writing the introduction. He did get to read a few of the first chapters, and he heard me teach part of a course on the joy of fathering at my church. He was proud that his son would take time from his career as an economist to undertake what he thought was a very important work.

My father, Charles Edward Hamrin Sr., passed away just six weeks shy of his eightieth birthday and nine months shy of celebrating his sixtieth anniversary with my mom, Violet, who still manages to carry on with the zest for life that has been her greatest gift to me.

I am so grateful that my dad demonstrated the basic elements of successful parenting: unconditional love, commitment, training by example, and the will to discipline. He showed me the tremendous value and importance of keeping the marriage solid. And most important, he left me a twelve-word statement that has guided me from the day in my youth when I first heard it: "Never put your final trust in people—put it only in God." Dad, I thank you for that verbal legacy and for your living legacy of loving God so faithfully, and loving Mom, my brother Charles Jr., and me unconditionally.

INTRODUCTION
EXPERIENCE
THE JOY

IF

• you feel that being a good father is the biggest, most important, and toughest job any man could have (which it probably is),

• you'd like to share in the type of pride that General Douglas MacArthur had: "By profession I am a soldier and take pride in that fact. But I am prouder—infinitely prouder—to be a father,"

• you have a desire to experience joy in being a father,

THEN this book is for you.

The key word above is desire. If you bring to this book a keen desire to be a great dad—a passion for excellence in fathering—I can assure you the book will help you attain this excellence. And through this commitment to fathering excellence, you will experience the incredible joy of fathering.

I'll warn you up front. This book is going to upset you, anger you, probably make you feel a bit guilty, and certainly challenge you. But it's also going to inspire you, give you hope, make you laugh, encourage you to be a great dad, and most of all give you practical suggestions about how to be a great dad.

The book in essence is a wake-up call to all fathers:

arise, take your fathering role seriously and joyfully, and in the process give your kids the gift they most desire and yourself the gift that will bring you inexpressible joy.

"Sounds great," you say. "But an economist writing a book on fathering?" Since that is probably on your mind, let's address it: Why is an economist—a practitioner of the dismal science—writing a book on fathering? And what can be gained from it?

As for the *why,* it boils down to this: I have many thoughts and deep convictions in my heart about both the responsibilities and the joys of being a father in today's world. I want to share these, not as expert to layman but simply as one dad to another— straight from a dad's heart. I also have two simple, yet profound people-related motivations:

> I want every father to experience the joy of fathering that I have experienced.
> I want every child to experience the unconditional love and active nurturing of the father.

Another type of motivation is society related: I deeply believe that many of the major societal ills we face in America today are due to the fact that fathers are not fulfilling their basic fathering responsibilities. A 1992 *Newsweek* article put it bluntly: "There is a high correlation between disrupted homes and just about every social problem imaginable." Put in a more positive light, fathers in America have the power to stay with their children and exercise their full range of fathering responsibilities; in so doing, they can alleviate many of the nation's most serious social problems. *Our effectiveness as fathers has a great deal to do with the strength of our society and America's longer-term future.*

As for the *what,* let's look first at what's in it for you—learning action steps to be a great dad and, through applying them, experiencing the joy of fathering.

In the past fifteen years, I have experienced incredible joy in my life in my role as father to my three kids—a deep-down satisfying, ongoing joy. And I want as many other men as possible to experience that same joy—starting now—so they won't miss out on it and so they can receive as much as they can while they can. Joy, happiness, satisfaction, fulfillment—call it what you like, but please recognize that it is to be found much more abundantly in your relationship with your kids than in your work.

Your children also have a lot to gain. All children need unconditional love and active nurturing from the father, not just from the mother. They may not show it or express it very well, but the evidence is overwhelming that every child has a deep heart-cry for the love and nurturing of a dad. This "father hunger," as the burgeoning men's movement calls it, is universal, and it will be filled in the next generation only by those of us who are fathers today. It really boils down to the basic point that our children *need* us dads and they *want* us dads.

OUR TREMENDOUS POWER

Whether you are a dad now or plan to be one, please realize that what's involved here is father power—the almost frightening degree of power we have as dads to fundamentally shape our children's lives. We don't have this much power in our jobs. We don't (or hopefully don't) have it with our wives. Nor do we have it with any other institutions or individuals we're involved with.

But rather than just offering my comments on this, I'm going to do what I will do frequently throughout the book: let the children speak. They are the experts I have paid the most attention to. If we're going to know what they need and want from us as dads and what kind of an impact we have on them, we've got to listen closely and carefully to them. For this reason, all direct words from children about their dads are in bold print.

I don't like my dad very much. Not once has he really hugged me. Rarely has he told me he loves me. I feel so awful because I can't ever run

to my dad and have him make things okay. I can never cry on my dad's shoulder. Not once has he ever said, "Julie, things will be okay." I want so badly to scream and let out all of this hurt. I feel so alone.[1]

That's one very negative form our father power can take. Here's the positive form:

The times that I remember best, though, are the times I spent with you. I love those memories best of all, Dad, and they're a big part of who I am. That's the whole point of these letters for me. My childhood is gone, and I will never be able to be with you the way I was with you as a little boy. I will never be that small, and you will never seem that big again. But I have my stories, and they comfort me when I am overwhelmed by the world, when I am too old all of a sudden, when I lose my sense of wonder. They are all I have of my boyhood, and the reason I wish we had spent more time together is that I wish I had more of them now. It isn't that you didn't do enough, you see, for I would always want more. You were the king of the world back then, the imp of fun, the man with all the answers, the one who could always fix what was broken. You made life seem magical to me.[2]

That was written by a twenty-six-year-old son. Isn't that what we all want to hear from our adult children? Don't we want them to look back to their childhood and youth and see a dad who was "king of the world" and "made life seem magical"?

OUR BASIC CHOICE

As these two stories illustrate, we're talking about power, but we're also talking about choice. Each of us in the role of father must choose how he is going to exercise that power.

Our basic choice is this: Do we invest ourselves in our kids, giving them the unconditional love and nurturing they need and deserve? Or do we invest our main energies in our work or elsewhere, demonstrate conditional love, and leave the nurturing to Mom—or to no one?

An old story illustrates our power and our responsibility so well:

> A smart-aleck ten-year-old came to a wise old man and wanted to make him stumble. The boy had a baby bird in his palm.
>
> Into a face highlighted with wisdom's wrinkles and crowned with gray hair, the boy poked his question: "Sir, is this bird in my hand dead or alive? Tell me, if you are so wise."
>
> Assured that the bird was alive, the old sage knew that if he said it was, the insensitive boy would crush it to death in his hand before opening his palm. If he said the bird was dead, the boy would let it fly away in freedom, but still mock him for his error.
>
> Looking steadily into the boy's cold eyes, the man said softly, "Son, it is as you will it."

Dad, it is as you will it. You can either crush your child or let your child soar.

Child soaring is what this book is all about. Each chapter contains principles and actions that will encourage your children to soar.

OUR VITAL CHALLENGE

Here's the vital challenge to dads: *Fathers in America must turn from their father-absence—whether the absence is physical, emotional, or spiritual—and begin to exercise their father power in positive, constructive ways in their children's lives.*

The evidence regarding father-absence is incontrovertible:

- Only 4 percent of teenage girls feel they could go to their fathers to talk about a serious problem.
- Seventh and eighth graders spend an average of 7.5 minutes a week in focused conversation with their fathers.
- When teens under stress were asked where they turn to for help in a crisis, dads were forty-eighth on the list.

The message these facts convey is quite sobering—dads in America just aren't a significant positive factor in their kids' lives. Yet the *absence* of father is having a major negative impact.

At the time America was founded, and for some time after that, fathers were the people primarily responsible for a child's intellectual and moral upbringing. As recently as fifty years ago, children spent three to four hours a day interacting with family members. Today, they spend fourteen and a half minutes, twelve of which are in the form of negative comments or reprimands.

Dads, we can do much better. We can offer our children unconditional love. We can actively nurture them. We can make life seem magical to them. And we can take the lead in building their character and forming their moral and spiritual values.

The challenge is great. But what challenge is more important to meet?

THE TWELVE KEYS TO JOY-FILLED FATHERING

As I said, my main purpose in writing this book is to help you experience the personal joy of fathering, and I do this by high-lighting twelve keys to joy-filled fathering. Where do these twelve keys—one per chapter—come from?

They come from two sources. The primary one is my many years of experience as father to my three kids. You should know, if you have read between the lines so far, that I have a passion for fathering. A passion is something that you want to experience a lot, to learn much about, to be good at. Friedrich Hegel, a great philosopher, said, "We may affirm absolutely that *nothing* great in the world has been accomplished without passion." This passion motivated me to leave my employment path of exciting jobs and steady paychecks nine years ago and become self-employed, pri-marily so I could spend time with my kids in their formative years.

The second major source is the experience of hundreds of peo-ple—people I know personally and those who have written of their experience. I've been a diligent student of good fathering practices, learning—from my friends, other adults, articles, books, and seminars— what kids desire in a father and what works. I was pleased to see that in many cases, what I observed in others or read about from others confirmed my personal experience.

Let's be clear about the value and merit of these steps—they are proven effective. I have seen them work in my home. They come from what kids say they desire in a dad and what their "great dad" does. They come from dads who state that they have worked in their homes. And they come from the experts who conduct interviews and surveys of fathers and kids.

The action steps and the suggestions in this book cover the basic foundation for being a great dad. They are quite comprehen-sive. But I do not claim that they cover all the steps involved in being a great dad. I offer them to you as a menu from which you can pick and choose those most applicable to your situation.

The book can be read from start to finish, but the chapters can also be used out of sequence. Different parts of the book may be important to you at different stages in your fathering experience. For instance, if your kids are six and eight today, chapter 5 on teenagers may not mean as much to you now as it almost certainly will in three to four years. At the end of each chapter is a "Points to Remember" list. It contains the main points and some practical tips from the chapter. This is for immediate review to help you decide where and how to start to improve your fathering.

A GUARANTEE FOR YOU

What kind of guarantee comes with these action steps? There is no guarantee that the conscientious practice of all of them will result in great kids. Too many other influential forces may lead kids astray. But it is fair to say that the more of them you conscientiously and effectively practice, the greater is the likelihood that your children will turn out to be well adjusted, with a positive outlook on life, and well equipped to handle the challenges of life. Thus, I can guarantee that you will be a great dad to the extent that you put these action steps effectively into play in your life. In short, you will have done your part. You will not have to face, at age sixty, the agonizing "if only" regrets that so many fathers have faced: "If only I had devoted more time and attention to my kids... told them I loved them more often... been there when they needed me."

START NOW AND PRESS ON

Let me share with you why I have such a sense of urgency about being a great dad. It arises directly from a fact that absolutely astounded me: *if you spend one hour per week in one-on-one time with a child, the total amount of time you will have with that child by the eighteenth birthday is only thirty-nine days.* Please read that again: thirty-nine days!

So we must start now to be great dads and to experience the joy of fathering. And we must endure in our quest to be great dads. It has been said that the difference between success and failure is that ability to hang in there five minutes longer. Well, there will be lots of times with a child that we'll be called upon to hang in there five minutes longer.

You don't sprint to become a great dad; you're running a marathon. Being a great dad requires commitment up front, patience during the race, and endurance to see your way to the finish line.

As in a marathon, every finisher is a winner.

MEET MY FAMILY

I would be remiss if I didn't introduce you to my wife and children since I will be referring to them throughout the book and they are my primary inspiration and "laboratory" in writing this book.

Carol, my wife and life partner, loves to read and think. She still must be coaxed into doing a variety of activities, but once "there," once "into it," she usually loves it and fully participates, whether it is skiing, golf, hiking, or going on one of our mini-escapes. Her sensitivity, compassion, and caring for others are evident. As a career China scholar, she's been working for almost twenty years—the last ten, part-time—at the U.S. Department of State, where she is now a senior researcher on Chinese affairs. For the past decade, she has been teaching at the School of Advanced International Studies of Johns Hopkins University. As president of her fan club, I think she knows contemporary China as well as anybody in this country. But most important, she knows her life's priorities and thus is a great mom to our three children.

Eric, our number one child (in birth order), is a "Renaissance man" who loves to engage in a wide variety of activities. Sports, piano, math, reading, geography, military history, anthropology, design, drawing, and roller-coasters—all have been a major passion at some point through the years. He usually excels at doing and learning. He also bears the burden of being a perfectionist and thus finds it difficult at times to enjoy his considerable accomplishments. What I think of most, however, when I think of Eric is moral integrity. He knows what is right and wrong, and he is tremendously sensitive to the wrong, both in his life and in the larger life swirling about him.

Krista, one of our twin daughters, calmly and effectively takes life as it comes to her. She exhibits great dedication and organization in her schoolwork, with high payoff in appreciation from teachers. Her leading talents (at least at this early stage of life) are in drawing and music, while she loves reading poetry and becoming "lost" in books. Her real gift, however, is dealing with people. Ever since she was very young, she has demonstrated a deep sensitivity to the feelings and needs of others.

Kira defines the word *dynamic*. Nothing is going to stop her from following her creative instincts and curiosities with considerable enthusiasm and energy. This trait shows up in excellent scholarship. Yet this same human dynamo was one of the sweetest four-year-old ballerinas ever. Dance is her major passion today. As Carol and I have often said, "If her talents and energies are rightly channeled, there will be no stopping her."

YOUR FATHERING LEGACY

No man counts himself great if his children have failed.
—SENECA

A FATHERING legacy. Your fathering legacy. If you're like I was or most men are, you have probably given little thought to your fathering legacy. Yet what could be more important in a man's life than what he bestows upon his children—what they have from him after he is gone?

I'm not talking about money, houses, cars, and other material possessions that are part of an estate. I'm talking primarily about memories and abilities, and about values and beliefs that shape the basic character and integrity of children. The way I picture it is this: I'm on my deathbed. I'm reviewing my life. What is it that I'm leaving my children of really lasting value? That's my fathering legacy.

What would you like your fathering legacy to be? I'd like you to give it some serious thought. Another way to think about it is to ask yourself, If I had the power to give each of my children one gift for life, what would it be?

THE POWER OF THE FATHERING LEGACY

Let's begin by witnessing the powerful impact a fathering legacy can have. After all, some men may protest, "Hey, I have only one kid. How significant can my fathering legacy be, particularly outside the confines of my family?" That's a good question, and a brief glimpse at Jonathan Edwards will provide an eloquent answer.

Jonathan Edwards, born in 1703, was a writer, theologian, pastor, and president of Princeton University. However, his greatest legacy by far was his fathering legacy. He committed himself to nurturing his eleven children. Every evening before dinner, Edwards gave his full attention to them for one hour. He also took one child along with him on out-of-town trips. In short, he invested himself in his children's lives. And the impact?

Of his known descendants,

- more than 300 became pastors, missionaries, or theological professors.
- 120 were professors at various universities.
- 110 became attorneys.
- 60 were prominent authors.
- 30 were judges.
- 14 served as presidents of universities and colleges.
- 3 served in the U.S. Congress.
- 1 became vice president of the United States.[1]

By committing himself to creating a positive fathering legacy, he not only helped his children, but he positively affected hundreds of his descendants and, through them, American society as a whole. A fathering legacy can have widespread ripples indeed.

Contrast the list of Edwards' descendants with the descendants of the Jukes family. Among the known descendants,

- 440 were physically wrecked by their own wickedness.
- 310 were professional paupers.
- 130 were convicted criminals.
- 60 were habitual thieves.
- 55 were victims of impurity.
- 7 were murderers.[2]

This type of negative legacy continues today. One frequent speaker at prisons asserted that he had not met one man in prison who had feelings of respect or affection for his father. Instead, feelings of hatred, resentment, and indifference express the full range of feelings toward fathers.

To sense the real power of a father's legacy, we need to see how one child views, and reacts to, a father's failed legacy. Here is a son's intimate portrait of what Robert Bly, one of the founders and leading figures of the modern men's movement, calls "a starvation in the cells for something only a father could give":

> **Dear Jim,**
> As for your concerns about Dad, that's a big issue and I'm not sure I know where to start. I can tell you that I have spent a long time in therapy dealing with it and am just now getting to some closure on it all. It has affected me a great deal, I know that for sure.... Dad is not going to change. I have had a hard time accepting that, and have spent my life setting myself up to receive some little acknowledgement or blessing from him only to be disappointed each time. Somewhere along the way I stopped trying. I will always miss him, though. There will always be a hollow place inside of me where love and acceptance from him should have been. That is some-

thing I can never change.... There is something he is afraid of: sharing, communicating, allowing another person to be okay, and respecting different opinions. Other ways of viewing life threaten him and so he cannot do that. Does he love us? Yes, in his own way. Is that enough for me? No, I need him to know and love me for the person I am.[3]

—*One brother to another about their dad*

This voice echoes what is in the hearts of many American men. A reporter at one of Bly's workshops described what happened after Bly spoke of this starvation in the cells.

Now, as more than a dozen men stand in line to kiss him goodbye, that hunger is almost palpable. Bly waits patiently, offering the unconditional embrace that these men, in their 30s and 40s, never felt from their own fathers. He throws his arms around each man, kisses him on the cheek and sends him on his way. Now, he is the father.

"All right," you say, "you've convinced me of the power inherent in a fathering legacy. I know I have this power. Now what do I do with it to leave my children and descendants a legacy that will be of positive benefit in their lives?"

In a nationwide survey of teens, what clearly emerged was a deep hunger for the bonds of love, affection, and good communication in the home to be the foundation for their lives.

LEGACIES CHILDREN WANT FROM THEIR FATHERS

This is a good place to turn to the kids to hear what they say they want from their parents. They are, after all, the ones who best know what they really need and desire.

Josh McDowell, the originator of that survey and a popular speaker on the problems of youths, relates a personal story that portrays the desire for love and affection:

It had been a very long speaking tour and I found myself in Phoenix, Arizona.... I had several high schools to cover that week, and one day I found it necessary to do an assembly outdoors at noon on the school lawn. This particular high school had an enrollment of about one thousand and it seemed as if almost every one of the kids had come out to sit on the grass and listen to some guy talk to them about sex.

I was that guy. Standing on a boulder to be seen and heard a little better, I began speaking on why so many young people trade sex in their search for true love and intimacy. Just as I got going, a group of punkers walked up and joined the crowd....

Twenty-two minutes later, I finished spelling out my thoughts on the difference between real love and the cheap substitute so many kids think they have to settle for in the back seat of a car. As I stepped down off the boulder, the leader of the punker group ran right up to me!

There, before the entire school assembly of almost a thousand kids, this husky young guy came within inches of my nose, so most of the crowd didn't really see or hear what happened next. They couldn't see the tears running down his cheeks or hear him ask me a poignant question:

"Mr. McDowell, would you give me a hug?"

Before I could even get my hands up to put my

arms around him, the big punker grabbed me in a bear hug, put his head on my shoulder, and started crying like a baby. I hugged him back and we stood there like that for what seemed to be over a minute. Just about any hug might seem long when it's from a big husky punker whose gold chains are imbedded in your chest. But I could see the kid was sincere. He wasn't putting me or the crowd on. He really wanted a hug!

Finally, the punker stepped back and said something that has become a typical statement from many teens: "Mr. McDowell, my father has never once hugged me or told me he loved me."[4]

I'll have a lot more to say about giving your kids all the love and affection you can, for that's where the fathering legacy begins.

After that foundation is laid, the building of the legacy relies heavily on communication with your children. Once again, Josh McDowell provides some disturbing, poignant feedback from teens—gathered at a conference for six hundred junior-high and high-school students—on the current status of father-child communication in America:

The number one question I heard that week was, "Josh, what can I do about my dad?"

"What do you mean?" I would ask.

"Well, he never talks to me. He never takes me anywhere. He never does anything with me."

I spoke sixteen times from Monday noon to Friday noon that week and had forty-two half-hour counseling sessions. I could have had three hundred if I had the time, but I handled all I could. At every one of these forty-two sessions, I asked the same question:

"Can you talk with your father?"

One student said yes. Forty-one said no.[5]

A legacy of providing your children what they most desire—love, affection, and communication—supplies all the basics. It certainly is a most worthy one to aim for.

Another legacy of utmost value is a lifestyle worthy of your children's emulation. Do you want your kids to have a certain character, integrity, guiding values? Then live your life accordingly. The way you live your life is your greatest opportunity to teach your kids what you would like them to be.

Chuck Swindoll, author of nearly two dozen books, credits his father with two great legacies, one of which was a morally pure lifestyle: "It never dawned on me that my father had one thought of unfaithfulness. And the modeling of purity of lips even though he worked around men that were vile and obscene really stuck."[6]

Incidentally, the second legacy Swindoll cites is an integral part of modeling what we wish our kids to become—how to properly treat a wife: "He really did honor my mom. I watched that on weekends. There were times they would have their rows, but I don't remember his ever raising his voice and certainly never his hand. So, I gained that kind of tenderness and consistency." The importance to the kids of the husband's proper treatment of his wife is well documented. A drop in parental harmony causes almost 60 percent of youths to report they feel like emotional orphans in their homes.

A BIG JOB AHEAD

Participants in the National Survey of Fathering were asked to rate the importance to them of 116 fathering practices and their own performance level in each area. Four areas consistently rated highest: (1) showing affection, (2) being a good example, (3) exhibiting parental togetherness, and (4) being spiritually mature. The sad fact is that they were the same areas in which the fathers rated their performance poorest. Dads, we've got a big job ahead.

Establishing these fathering legacies is going to require a true liberation for many middle-aged, middle-class men.

They must give themselves permission to stop striving so hard, for so long, at their jobs; permission to invest in experiences and relationships, not things; permission to live life at a slower pace and be more available and open to the kids. The words below focus on living life over again but they can apply as well to the rest of our lives as we proceed to establish our fathering legacy:

> If I had my life to live over again, I'd try to make more mistakes next time.
>
> I would relax, I would limber up, I would be sillier than I have been this trip.
>
> I know of very few things I would take seriously.
>
> I would take more trips, I would be crazier.
>
> I would climb more mountains, swim more rivers, and watch more sunsets.
>
> I would do more walking and looking.
>
> I would eat more ice cream and less beans.
>
> I would have more actual troubles, and fewer imaginary ones.
>
> You see, I'm one of those people who lives life prophylactically and sensibly hour after hour, day after day.
>
> Oh, I've had my moments, and if I had to do it over again, I'd have more of them.
>
> In fact, I'd try to have nothing else, just

moments, one after another, instead of living so many years ahead each day.

I've been one of those people who never go anywhere without a thermometer, a hot-water bottle, a gargle, a raincoat, aspirin, and a parachute.

If I had to do it over again I would go places, do things, and travel lighter than I have.

If I had my life to live over, I would start barefooted earlier in the spring and stay that way later in the fall.

I would play hooky more.

I wouldn't make such good grades, except by accident.

I would ride on more merry-go-rounds.

I'd pick more daises. I'd enjoy my sons every day.[7]

—Anonymous

Loosening up is important. But at the same time, you need to establish specific goals for the fathering legacy you wish to give your children. One way is to picture each of your children five years from now. Now think of three things you would like to have accomplished with each of them by then. Then list the steps you should take to achieve this objective.

Another way is to list the five most important values you want each of your children to have for life. Then ask yourself, What am I doing to foster honesty and trust (and other values) in their lives? Ask, In the past week, what specifically did I do with my children to instill any one of the five values? And keep asking yourself such questions.

These goals you set for your fathering legacy involve one of the few areas in your life that you cannot delegate to another. A fathering legacy, by definition, is the sole responsibility of the father.

In thinking of this awesome responsibility of establishing a fathering legacy, I am reminded of Edmund Burke's famous statement:

I am one
I am only one
But I am one
I cannot do everything
But I can do something
What I can I will do
I am one

POINTS TO REMEMBER

- What would you like your fathering legacy to be? That's one of the most significant questions you face as a father.
- A fathering legacy can have widespread ripples across society and down through the ages in your descendants.
- Consider "a starvation in the cells for something only a father could give."
- Kids want most of all—in essence the primary fathering legacy—the bonds of love, affection, and communication in the home as the foundation for their lives.
- "My father has never once hugged me or told me he loved me."
- Another legacy is to have a lifestyle worthy of your children's emulation.
- Children want and need the legacy of how to properly treat and honor one's wife.
- Give yourself permission to stop striving so hard for so long; to invest in experiences and relationships, not things; to live life a lot more open to the kids.
- You cannot delegate the goals you set for your fathering legacy.
- "I am only one / But I am one.

PART ONE
BEING THERE

This part of the book discusses the starting point for all of us fathers: being there. If we are not there, all the wonderful character-building practices described in Part 2 can't take place. Each of them involves spending time with each child. We can't build character from afar.

They also can't take place if we are not "there" for our children while they are young, because they aren't going to listen to us or respect our views when they move into the adolescent-teen years.

That is why the very first chapter begins with the most fundamental action step: spelling love T-I-M-E. All kids want love, but they don't want it as mere words from us, as some principle they're supposed to assume. No, kids of all ages want love expressed as time spent with them. As one father said to his children when they were visiting the old homestead where he grew up: "Kids, what I remember most about the holidays is that my dad was there. Nothing spectacular, he was just there."

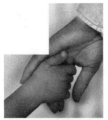

CHAPTER 1

SPELLING LOVE
T-I-M-E

The greatest of
all sacrifices...
is the sacrifice of
time.
—PLUTARCH

CHILDREN spell love T-I-M-E. It's as simple as that and as profound as that. There's no way of getting around this basic fact. The myth that brief, sporadic quality time can make up for lack of time—a concept closely tied to the yuppie acquisitiveness drive of the 1980s—doesn't cut it. One can't just manufacture quality moments, saying, "Now we're going to have quality moments." No, it is out of quantity time—being there with your kids a lot—that the quality moments will come. This century will see the reemergence of a time-honored truth: quantity time with their parents is what children desire and what they need.

I like these statements on the critical importance of time that I've come across in parenting books:

"Time is the very crucible of fathering."

"The saying 'Time is of the essence' can be rephrased slightly to describe strong family life. Time *is* the essence."

"Time provides the framework for all elements of family success—communication, discipline, values."

I feel fortunate in having learned this fundamental great dad practice in my early days of being a father. Indeed, it became so important to me that it caused me to quit a presidential campaign job at age thirty-six and become self-employed. I wanted to spend a lot of time with my kids while they were still young.

How did I become so deeply committed to spending time with my three kids that I was willing to leave a series of prestigious, well-paying jobs for a "going solo" career that caused a drop in income, security, and reputation? There were two motivating forces.

One was the words I heard from a man I deeply respect and admire. He is Richard Halverson, former chaplain of the U.S. Senate (1981-95) and, before that, my pastor at Fourth Presbyterian Church. On a retreat for young couples, he said that the main thing he regretted was that he did not spend enough time at home with his kids when they were young. "I'll never forget," he said, "the words of my five-year-old daughter: 'Daddy, how come you're hardly ever home with us?'" Why those words hit me so hard, penetrated to my inner being, and stuck with me I'll never know. But they did. And I resolved then and there that at a minimum, none of my children would have to say those words.

The other force was the song "Cat's in the Cradle." It's not just a song—it's an anthem for dads everywhere. It should come with a label: "WARNING—listening to this song will be hard on your psyche. Be prepared for some serious soul-searching."

I offer the words of this song in grateful appreciation to Harry Chapin and Sandy Chapin with the hope that its message can touch a few more hearts:

Cat's in the Cradle

My child arrived just the other day;
he came to the world in the usual way.
But there were planes to catch and bills to pay;
he learned to walk while I was away.
And he was talking 'fore I knew it,
and as he grew he'd say,
I'm gonna be like you, Dad,
you know I'm gonna be like you.

And the cat's in the cradle and the silver spoon,
little boy blue and the man in the moon.
"When you comin' home, Dad'" "I don't know when,
but we'll get together then;
you know we'll have a good time then."
My son turned ten just the other day;
he said, "Thanks for the ball, Dad,
come on let's play.
Can you teach me to throw?"
I said, "Not today,
I got a lot to do."
He said, "That's okay."
And he walked away,
but his smile never dimmed,
it said, "I'm gonna be like him, yeah,
you know I'm gonna be like him."

And the cat's in the cradle and the silver spoon,
little boy blue and the man in the moon.
"When you comin' home, Dad'" "I don't know when,
but we'll get together then;
you know we'll have a good time then."

Well, he came from college just the other day;
so much like a man I just had to say,
"Son, I'm proud of you, can you sit for awhile?"
He shook his head and he said with a smile,
"What I'd really like, Dad, is to borrow the car keys;
see you later, can I have them please?"

And the cat's in the cradle and the silver spoon,
little boy blue and the man in the moon.
"When you comin' home, Son'" "I don't know when,
but we'll get together then;
you know we'll have a good time then."

I've long since retired, my son's moved away;
I called him up just the other day.
I said, "I'd like to see you if you don't mind."
He said, "I'd love to, Dad, if I can find the time.
You see, my new job's a hassle and the kids have the flu,
but it's sure nice talkin' to you, Dad,
it's been sure nice talkin' to you."
And as I hung up the phone, it occurred to me,
he'd grown up just like me;
my boy was just like me.

And the cat's in the cradle and the silver spoon,
little boy blue and the man in the moon.
"When you comin' home, Son?" "I don't know when,
but we'll get together then, Dad,
we're gonna have a good time then."

"Cat's in the Cradle" by Harry Chapin and Sandy Chapin
copyright © 1974 Story Songs Ltd.

Here's one son's "dad coming home" story that expresses what goes on in the hearts and minds of thousands of children:

Dad Coming Home Was the Real Treat
by Howard Mann

When I was a little boy I never left the house without kissing my parents goodbye.

I liked kissing my mother because her cheek felt mushy and warm, and because she smelled of peppermints. I liked kissing my father because he felt rough and whiskery and smelled of cigars and witch hazel.

About the time I was 10 years old, I came to the conclusion that I was now too big to kiss my father. A mother, OK. But with a father, a big boy should shake hands—man to man, you see.

He didn't seem to notice the difference or to mind it. Anyway, he never said anything about it. But then he never said much about anything, except his business.

In retrospect, I guess it was also my way of getting even with him. Up until then, I had always felt I was something special to him. Every day, he would come home from that mysterious world of his with a wondrous treat, just for me. It might be a miniature baseball bat, engraved with Babe Ruth's signature. It might be a real honeycomb with waffle-like squares soaked in honey. Or it might be exotic rahat, the delectable, jellied Turkish candies, buried in powdered sugar and crowded into a little wooden crate.

How I looked forward to his coming home

each night! The door flung open and there he stood. I would run to him, hug him while he lifted me high in his arms.

I reached my peak the day of my seventh birthday. I woke up before anyone else in the family and tiptoed into the dining room. There, on the heavy mahogany table, was a small, square wristwatch with a brown leather strap, stretched out full length in a black velvet box. Could it really be for me? I picked it up and held it to my ear. It ticked! Not a toy watch from the 5-and-10, but a real watch like grown-ups wore. I ran into his bedroom, woke up father and covered him with kisses. Could any boy possibly be as happy as me?

Later, it began to change. At first, I wasn't aware it was happening. I supposed I was too busy with school and play and having to make new friends all the time. (We moved every two years, always seeking a lower rent.)

The flow of treats dried up. No more bats or honeycombs. My father gradually disappeared from my life. He would come home late, long after I had gone to sleep. And he would come home with his hands empty. I missed him very much, but I was afraid to say anything. I hoped that he would come back to me as strangely as he had left. Anyhow, big boys weren't supposed to long for their fathers.

Years after he died, my mother talked about how the Depression had "taken the life out of him." It had crushed his dream of being a "big man." He no longer had money for treats. He no longer had time for me.

I am sorry now. I look at his picture and his crinkly hazel eyes and wish that he were here today. I would tell him what is happening with me now and talk about things that he might like to hear—politics, foreign events and how business is doing. And I would put my arms around his neck and say, "Pop, you don't have to bring me any-thing—just come home early."

And I would kiss him.[1]

TODAY'S ABSENT FATHERS

How many men are living out the Chapins' song right now? Precise numbers aren't available, but all the evidence points to far too many. The fathers in one study estimated that they spent fif-teen to twenty minutes a day with each of their kids. Microphones attached to the children showed that the average amount of time was thirty-seven seconds per day. Another study found that the average American father gives only thirty-five sec-onds of undivided attention to a child each day. Meanwhile, that child spends thirty to fifty hours a week watching TV. Focusing on fathers per se, American children spend ten times as many hours with TV males and TV dads as they do their own fathers.

Those are the facts. Erma Bombeck, noted for her outrageous (but perceptive) humor, gives us a nonhumorous portrait of what life was like with a father who didn't spend much time with his child:

One morning my father didn't get up and go to work. He went to the hospital and died the next day.

I hadn't thought that much about him before. He was just someone who left and came home and seemed glad to see everyone at night. He opened the jar of pickles when no one else could. He was the only one in the house who wasn't afraid to go into the basement by himself.

He cut himself shaving, but no one kissed it or got excited about it. It was understood when it rained, he got the car and brought it around to the door. When anyone was sick, he went out to get the prescription filled. He took lots of pictures.... but he was never in them.

Whenever I played house, the mother doll had a lot to do. I never knew what to do with the daddy doll, so I had him say, "I'm going off to work now," and threw him under the bed.

The funeral was in our living room and a lot of people came and brought all kinds of good food and cakes. We never had so much company before.

I went to my room and felt under my bed for the daddy doll. When I found him, I dusted him off and put him on my bed.

He never did anything. I didn't know his leaving would hurt so much.[2]

Why can't dads understand that children want their time and attention? A substantial part of the reason is that so many of them do not have a good role model to follow. Their dads simply weren't there for them. Survey after survey levies this indictment. One was a survey of 370 men who graduated from Harvard in the mid-1960s, men who are the "success stories" of our society. Summing up his research, Samuel Osherson says, "The interviews that I have had with men in their thirties and forties convince me that the psychological or physical absence of fathers from their families is one of the underestimated tragedies of our times."[3] Osherson cites similar results from other surveys.

Psychologist Jack Sternbach, who examined the father-son relationship in seventy-one of his clients, found that

> fathers were physically absent for 23 percent of the men; 29 percent had psychologically absent fathers who were too busy with work, uninterested in their sons, or passive at home; 18 percent had psychologically absent fathers who were austere, moralistic, and emotionally uninvolved; and 15 percent had fathers who were dangerous, frightening to their son, and seemingly out of control. Only 15 percent of Sternbach's cases showed evidence of fathers appropriately involved with their sons.[4]

And in an interview with successful businessmen, scientists, and scholars, all males age forty-seven, George Valliant found that "in more than ninety-five percent of the cases, fathers were either cited as negative examples or were mentioned as those who were not influences."[5]

The adverse impact of absent fathers on kids is unmistakable. In the 1980s, estimates were that eight to ten million children suffered from emotional disorders or experienced developmental difficulties. According to E. Kent Hayes, who has worked with the children of disrupted families for over twenty-five years, among all his startling discoveries one essential factor remains constant: "Parental neglect is the primary force promoting the evolution of today's disturbed child."

The problem of father-absence has devastating effects on the children involved and also carries heavy costs for society. Because of the tripling of the divorce rate and quadrupling of the out-of-wedlock birthrate since the 1950s, men between ages twenty and forty-nine spend an average of only seven years living in a home with young children, a decline of nearly 50 percent in the past fifty years. The results? A child in a female-headed household is six times more likely to be poor than a child in a two-parent family. More than 70 percent of youths in juvenile correctional facilities come from fatherless homes, as do more than 80 percent of adolescents in psychiatric hospitals.

SOME FIRST PRINCIPLES ON T-I-M-E

Okay. Enough of the problems. What is the solution?

I have a whole series of very practical "to do's" to share with you. But before I turn to them, I want to present some critical principles regarding fathering and time.

- *A child cherishes a father's presence above all else.*
- *You have a very short time in which to be the major influence on your children's lives.*
- *Little Time = Little Influence*
- *You can't buy back lost time.*
- *The world, deadlines, contracts, and so forth will always be there—your children won't.*
- *You can never spend too much time with your family.*
- *The thief in American homes today is overactivity.*
- *Whatever intimacy parents and teens enjoy is almost always cultivated before the age of twelve—rarely after it.*
- *Out of quantity time come the quality moments.*
- *If you make time with children when they're young, there will be opportunities and even requests from them when they're older.*
- *If you hear, you forget. If you see, you remember. If you do you understand.*
- *There really comes such a time as too late.*

I trust that these principles have inspired a commitment to spending time with your kids. Now, what can you do? What are good first steps?

ACTION STEPS FOR SPELLING LOVE T-I-M-E

The best first step is to plan the time you will have together with the kids. Block it out on your schedule.

Include your family in your date book. You use time management skills on the job. Why not at home? Perhaps you'll want to make it a set period each day or a set period—maybe two to four hours each weekend. Whatever time you choose, get it on the schedule or it is likely to fade quickly from the agenda. And don't forget to share your schedule with your wife.

One action step that I have taken is to keep a list of mini-adventures on hand. Mini-adventures are one- or two-day excursions (usually on weekends) to nearby places that would be exciting for the kids.

The concept cropped up one day when I was scanning through some brochures about sights in and around the Washington, D.C., area. I realized that we could miss out on some neat things if I didn't list them and plan a few into each year. So I developed the list and tried to include things that were either low cost or no cost to fight—on behalf of my kids, our values, and our budget—the rampant commercialism in our society. Fortunately, the idea has largely worked because each of my kids is not demanding at all about buying things or spending much money at such places as amusement parks. In fact, they take a healthy pride in their frugality.

I developed the list almost seven years ago. Recently, I took inventory of how well we've been doing. Of the one-day adventures, we have gone on ten of the sixteen listed. These have included outings to Baltimore's inner harbor, the Virginia state fair, and the Bluemont Fair.

The batting average on the two-day excursions is nowhere near as good: five out of twenty. One, however, became a real winner: the cabin we go to each fall at Cacapon State Park. Just to give you some idea of these excursions, here are a few in the still-to-do category: hiking in the George Washington National Forest; riding the Cass Scenic Railroad (an old steam locomotive train in the mountains of West Virginia, and taking a white-water raft trip. I can't wait!

Once you have a time blocked out and you have set your priorities, then think, *Nothing is going to keep me from this time, whether it be a football game on TV or the president calling.* Make sure your kids aren't so overprogrammed that their activities rob you of time together. Without this mind-set, other good activities will eat away at your dedicated times. In life, the "good" often crowds out the "best."

Another action step is to take some time to discover what each child is "into" currently and then share that interest. For instance, this past year my son has had a passion for roller-coasters. So I planned a weekend trip to an amusement park near Pittsburgh that has the tallest and fastest roller-coaster. Needless to say, the trip was a smashing success. But I also want to emphasize the enjoyment—free of charge—of giving Eric my ear while he talks about coasters, helping him write for literature and find books about them, and praising the scale-model coaster he created on our Ping-Pong table.

You should try to avoid the type of situation retold by Josh McDowell:

> "I offered to take my kid out to have a good time, but he didn't have any fun at all—the whole thing was a big failure."

> "What did you do with him?" I wondered.

"Well, I love to golf, so I took him golfing," the dad said insistently. "It turns out he hates golfing, so I guess that's that."[6]

Operating with a self-focused philosophy will lead to a lot of "that's that" situations. Remember, focus on their interests—their world—not yours. Your children will appreciate it.

> **They, God love them, always seemed to have time for me or to take themselves away from what they were doing for me and the interests I had. I kind of wish I knew then what I know now because I didn't appreciate them like I should have. I kind of feel sorry for my friends because their parents were always "too busy" to get involved in their interests, whereas I can't say that I didn't have at least two fans at every one of my sporting events or class performances.**[7]

Dads who travel have it particularly rough, but some creative solutions exist. One is to take a child along. It can't be done, you feel. Listen to Tony Campolo, a professor and speaker who's constantly on the road: "I would strongly recommend what we did to any parent who is torn between the need to be with his or her children, on the one hand, and extensive travel demands on the other. Taking you [his son] on the road with me allowed us some of the best quality time we ever had together."[8]

Another idea for the traveling dad is to do fun activities when you are at home with the family. Do you like tennis? Play with the family or at least one member who likes tennis. Do you like to swim? Swim with the family. In other words, dedicate your at-home activities to the family as much as possible. And when you settle in on the plane home or begin the drive back in your car, start thinking of the family. Determine to leave the business matters behind, and refocus on what you can do with your wife and kids.

Want to get really radical about spending enough time with your kids? Take a firm stance on not working during key family hours, such as nights or weekends. Consider the commitment of this father, a photographer who was in great demand and thus traveled often:

> To maintain some balance between his demanding career and a family he loved deeply, the man had identified and tenaciously adhered to a particular value—he refused to work on weekends. Whether commissioned to photograph a rock star, the president, or the queen of England, if the job involved a weekend, he simply said no. He had vowed that weekends would be devoted to his family, and he refused to make exceptions.[9]

An absolute must is to spend one-on-one time with each child. Once a week would be great, and once a month would be better than most dads manage. One-on-one time, regardless of what's done, tells each child, "I think you're special. I want to spend time with you." In general, one-on-one time often affords those rare moments when kids can really share what's on their hearts.

Here's a fresh idea that should get an energetic response from your kids. Tell each one, "I'm going to give you thirty (sixty or ninety) minutes of my time today (or this week). You choose what you want to do." That's probably one of the greatest gifts you could give them, and as the phrase goes, it's "a gift that keeps on giving." A great story illustrates how kids can easily recognize that this is a gift that "keeps on giving" even while the father can't:

> It is said of Boswell, the famous biographer of Samuel Johnson, that he often referred to a special day in his childhood when his father took him fishing. The day was fixed in his adult mind, and he often reflected upon many of the things his father had taught him in the course of their fishing experience together. After having heard of that particular excursion so often, it occurred to someone much later to check the journal that Boswell's father kept and determine what had been said about the fishing trip from the parenting perspective. Turning to that date, the reader found only one sentence entered: "Gone fishing today with my son; a day wasted."[10]

I have enjoyed taking each of my children to a restaurant. The practice began one day when Eric and I happened to be near Chesapeake Bay Seafood House around lunchtime. Knowing that it was his favorite eating establishment, I surprised him by pulling in. The notion of dining just with Dad caught his fancy, so he promoted the idea of having another one. I said, "Oh, you mean another men-only lunch." That really clicked with him, and we've had several lunches and breakfasts together.

I believe the reaction to this lunch from one of my daughters went something like this: "That's not fair. I want to have one of those." After some gentle teasing on my part about how it would be impossible for her to go on a "men-only" lunch with me, I assured her and her sister that I wanted instead to have "daughter dates" with each of them. They loved the idea.

Now, we're not talking elegant here. Or high finances. This is one time in your life when you can safely make the extravagant promise, "You name it. I'll take you there." And when you're at McDonald's, your bigheartedness can continue with, "You can have anything you want." It's wonderful to see her face light up when she says, "Really? Even a milk shake?" and you say, "Yes, even a milk shake."

I should add that Carol and her daughters have girls' nights out, too. In fact, you and your wife can "specialize" in these events. For example, I share sports and coasters with Eric; Carol is his mentor in marathon discussions of history and world events and still beats him in backyard minigolf.

Here's a helpful list of one-on-one activities cited by the one hundred exceptional families highlighted in *Back to the Family:*

- Whenever a young child shows you proudly what she did—a puzzle, a picture, a house of blocks—ask her if she'd like to do it again so you can watch.
- While you are enjoying a hobby—gardening, woodworking, crafts, painting—invite a child to watch and introduce him to the basics.
- Use a tape recorder to produce a sound diary for each child. Record his earliest sounds—laughing, cooing, crying. Continue with his first words, songs, counting. In essence, create a permanent time capsule of his development through language.
- Take a child to visit your workplace. If possible, let him spend time with you as you move through your day. Indeed, the chance to "see where Mom/Dad works" was ranked at or near the top of favorite parent-child activities by these children.[11]

If at times you get discouraged and think it's just too tough to carve out the time for one-on-one interaction, think of Susanna Wesley who, in addition to being the mother of John and Charles Wesley, one the founder of the Methodist church and the other a prolific hymn writer, was mom to seventeen other kids. She gave each child at least an hour a week of individual time. Now that's spelling love T-I-M-E.

POINTS TO REMEMBER
- Quantity time with their parents is what children desire and what they need.
- The five-year-old said, "Daddy, how come you're hardly ever home with us?"
- Survey after survey has pointed to fathers who seemingly can't find the time to be with their children.
- A child cherishes a father's presence above all else.
- The world, deadlines, contracts, and so on will always be there—your children won't.
- The best first step is to plan the time you will have together with your kids. Block it out on your schedule.
- Take some time to discover what each child is "into" currently and then share it.
- For dads who travel, take a child along; begin focusing on family activities on your way home.
- Spend one-on-one time with each child, which conveys, "I think you're special. I want to spend time with you."
- Take a firm stance on *not* working during key family hours, such as nights or weekends.

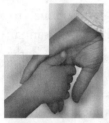

CHAPTER 2

SEIZING THE MOMENT

Life is either a
daring adventure
or nothing at all.
—HELEN KELLER

THIS CHAPTER focuses on a theme that characterizes my life—a zest for living. So much of the joy of fathering comes in the little moments tucked into each and every day, not necessarily the big planned events or annual family vacations. All we as dads have to do is to adopt Helen Keller's perspective on living, seeing each day as an opportunity for creative new ventures with our kids that will infuse them with an enthusiasm for life. Seize the moment!

A hallmark of a dad who can seize many moments with his kids is spontaneity. You can't easily plan seized moments. I like a line from a Jackson Browne song that goes, "The times we were most happy were the times we never tried." Seized moments are like that—moments that just happen, often on a whim. We probably won't know what to expect, but that's half the fun.

Spontaneity also speaks powerfully to our kids. A teenage girl told how loved she felt when her parents changed their evening plans after seeing her sadness over some troubles with friends at school—just to be nearby in case she wanted to talk.

Be spontaneous. And be present focused. It's impossible to seize the moment if you are always worried about or planning for the future. As Paul Tournier says,

"Most people spend their entire lives indefinitely preparing to live."

Look upon each new day with eager anticipation for the surprises it may hold.

When you become present focused, you can easily see pockets of time with your kids that you can creatively fill. Many ideas presented in this chapter take less than five minutes; some, less than a minute. As you fill each of these pockets of time with some fun activity or caring words, you are sending an unsaid but very clear "I love you" message to your children. Even very young children can sense this message, as this memory of a walk with his dad when the boy was only four shows:

> Magic warmed the English damp as we ambled hand in hand through his favorite woodland. He would grip my hand and point when he saw a rabbit or bird, and I would quiver in silent ecstasy as I saw it too. But the greatest miracle of all was an acorn. He showed me how you could take it out of the cup and how you could put it back again. His hand was big and the acorn small.
>
> Why is the memory vivid? Why are my emotions powerfully stirred by so trivial a matter? I have no idea. I only know that none of his

impatience with me during the years that followed ever erased it. When I try to think of a specific instance of his impatience, I'm at a loss to do so. Yet my mind ever comes to rest on the joy of that particular walk.[1]

INSIDE THE HOME

In the past twenty-seven hours, I have seized the moment in three different ways. The first was last evening when Kira and Krista were practicing their piano duet. As they came to the big finish, my thunderous applause suddenly sounded from afar, accompanied by "bravo, bravo." It was a simple, brief expression that I enjoy their piano playing.

The second came at breakfast this morning when Kira plunked herself on my lap. Often this occurs at what is not exactly the most convenient or opportune time—like when I am relaxing with a cup of coffee or still eating my bowl of fruit. So the natural reaction is, "Wait. Can't you see I'm not finished yet?" But I never say that, for I realize the tremendous importance of this relationship with a daughter at the outset of her adolescent years. Chances are that next year, she won't think of sitting on my lap. So I'm going to let myself be "inconvenienced" all she wants as I soak up these special moments with my daughter.

The third moment also involved Kira, which reminds me that these moments usually come in cycles, changing in nature and intensity with each child at each stage of life. Right now happens to be Kira's season with Daddy. I read somewhere that the moments of sending your children off to school and of welcoming them home are ones that can be particularly special. So I try to send each child off to school with an enthusiastic "Have a great day" and a kiss for each daughter. Kira and I add a little ritual. As soon as she gets onto our driveway, she faces me, and we both begin waving. We keep it up as she backs up the driveway and goes past the mailbox to the "sign-off" point where we vigorously wave and then turn around to face our respective days. I know that the picture of my daughter waving to me as she haltingly backs up the driveway will be forever etched in my memory. And I imagine she'll see her daddy waving by the front door window for some time in her mind's eye as well.

Not very big deals, are they? But, oh, how wonderful to have such pockets of love and joy to make each day a bit special.

Here's a handy tip for seizing the moment even when you're tired or grumpy and don't feel like it at all. When your child asks you to do something at such a moment, before saying no or later, just look right into the face of your child for five seconds. That's all—five seconds— and see the result. One dad describes what happened when he withheld the instant no he wanted to give:

> I had just buried myself in the newspaper when Aaron flew into the house screaming, "Daddy's home! Daddy's home!" He leaped into my lap, shoved the paper aside, grabbed my face so that I had to look him in the eye, and said, "Hi, buddy! Want to play?"
>
> I didn't. But I couldn't remember the last time I'd taken time to play with him. So down went the paper, and off went the set. Out came the stack of children's books, and for the 937th time we laughed our way through Go, Dog, Go.
>
> Aaron's too young to realize how tiring a job can be. He doesn't even comprehend what kinds of things a pastor has to do. But he does understand that when a dad loves his son he is willing to read books to him.
>
> Later I grabbed a bite to eat and headed out the door to my meeting. "Bye, Daddy," he called. "I

love you very, very much."

I felt greatly refreshed.[2]

I especially treasure two "moment seizers" of the past. One involved dancing with Krista or Kira in my arms when they were four and five years old. I'd hear a pretty song playing, and I'd pick one of them up and dance one or two minutes, hugging my precious little girl who in turn was resting her head on Daddy's shoulder.

The other involved the many, many moments I've shared with Eric centered on his various passions. When it was geography at age six, I'd often be quizzed by him on where some remote city was on the globe, or I'd listen to him as he rattled off the 126 countries he knew. When it was G.I. Joe at age nine, I'd frequently listen as he detailed the most recent battles between Cobra and the Joes, or I'd visit one of his fort sites in our woods. When it was military history at age twelve, I'd look at his lists of all the military battles that took place between 700 and 1300 A.D. . And when it was roller-coasters at age fourteen, I listened to him reel off the statistics on how many rides he has had in his life and answered his questions, such as "What are your five favorite wooden roller coasters?"

As I look back on all these pockets of time, my basic impression is that about 70 percent were generally enjoyable while 30 percent were somewhat tedious and interest had to be summoned from deep within. But the key point is this: I spent time on all these "pockets" because I recognized that these were ongoing points of real connection and relationship building with my son whose life for twelve- to eighteen-month periods tends to focus on a single, all-consuming passion.

I really have learned interesting things from Eric about geography, fossils, military history, and roller-coasters (though I'm still not sure about G.I. Joe).

> *It is all part of entering their world, which can often be unexpect-*
> *edly pleasant when you do it with an open mind and heart.*

You can do all sorts of creative things with kids, ranging from the wild and wacky to the more serious and meaningful. Here are some I've heard and read about:

Wild and Wacky Moments with the Kids

- Have dinner in the bedroom—tablecloth and all.
- Have a "Tom Jones" dinner, where no utensils can be used (this had best be in the kitchen).
- Have a meal where everyone must eat with the less-dexterous hand.
- Wear yourself out wrestling with your kid on the family room floor.
- Throw a special "Celebrate Monday" party with favorite foods and desserts just to show your kids you care about them.
- Let your children be the dad or mom at a meal.
- Tell one child, "Tonight I'm yours. What do you want to do?"

More Serious, Meaningful Moments with the Kids

- Invite your children to help you plan a special surprise for Mom—a nice meal, a "Mom Appreciation Night," and so on.
- Write a note to each child and mail it.
- Get out the family photo album and reminisce about your childhood or the kids' when they were babies and toddlers.
- Have family members write in one hundred words or less what their family is all about—as if they were telling a new

friend about their family for the first time.

- Ask each family member to share one good thing of the day at dinner.
- Show your children special love and care when they are sick.

One final suggestion: always try to respond to a child's initiatives. Just keep in mind that relationship is more important than smooth gravy:

> One evening my friend Marilyn was in the midst of preparing gravy for dinner when her teenage son rushed into the kitchen shouting, "Mom, come outside quickly. I've got something to show you."
>
> There is a critical point in the preparation of gravy when it must be stirred in order to have a smooth consistency. Marilyn, who is a gourmet cook and relishes the thought of a perfect dinner, was at that critical preparation point and almost said, "Can't you wait a minute? I've got to finish stirring the gravy." But an inner sense said, "Go." After all, it had been weeks since her son had asked her anything—or even wanted to be with the family. So she turned off the stove, removed the gravy, and went outside. Her son pointed to the western horizon and exclaimed, "Mom, look at that sunset. Isn't that the most beautiful thing you have ever seen?" They both watched until the last rays disappeared.[3]
>
> A wasted moment? It may have seemed so if smooth gravy is the thing you value most in your life. But as this mother said, "I'd eat lumpy gravy

every night of the week to have that kind of daily experience with my teenager. After all, gravy soon disappears, but the relationship I establish with my son can last a lifetime."

THE OUTDOORS

I'm a real outdoors fanatic, so I try to do as many things outdoors with my kids as possible. Three special seized moments come to mind immediately.

Monday afternoon outings are first. Elementary schools in our county close at 1:15 on Mondays, which gives a dad with a flexible work schedule a wonderful opportunity to do some fun things with his kids when there aren't so many people around. Usually, it would be a hike in the woods or a trip to nearby Burke Lake to visit the playground and toss the football around.

"Snow days" have offered another break from school, which we have always taken full advantage of. Recognizing how few and far between these are in the Washington, D.C., area, Carol often takes the day off, and we always make it a point to get out there first thing in the morning when the snow is fresh to coast down the hills in our yard and neighborhood. Carol taught the kids a favorite—making snow ice cream.

When the girls were five, I spent a sunny summer afternoon taking them to the Junior Olympics. Kira entered the dashes, and Krista entered the softball throw and the "hang." Kira just missed the medals, but Krista ended up with the gold in both of her events. No parent of a real Olympic gold medal winner has been prouder than I was when Krista went up and had those medals draped around her neck. It was a very special moment (I almost could hear "The Star Spangled Banner" playing in the distance). But it was surpassed five minutes later when Krista took off one of the medals and put it around Kira's neck so she could have one, too. *That* is what the joy of fathering is all about.

One thing I haven't yet done is to say to one of my children right before bedtime, "Come outside with me." There, in the backyard, will be a campsite all ready for an evening under the stars with Dad. Two different experiences I've read about highlighted the significance of such an evening. The first is about a father and his seven-year-old son:

> On an August night, the father bundled up the sleeping child and carried him out into the darkness. As the boy's sleep-filled eyes began to focus on his surroundings, his father shouted, "Look!" And there in the sky the little boy saw a star leap from its place and fall toward the ground. Then incredibly, another star fell, and another and another. That was all. But the boy never forgot that night when his father did the unexpected, and he determined that he would do the same some August evening when his boy was seven.[4]

The other story is told by Joni Eareckson Tada, a woman who broke her neck as a teenager in a diving accident that left her paralyzed from the shoulders down. She relates how when she was five years old, her passion was to snuggle next to her dad on the back porch, watch the moon rise, and then name all the constellations in the summer sky. From these times, she "learned early what passion and wonder are all about."[5]

But my favorite story, related by Bruce Larson, involves the wild and crazy antics of a dad who knew what seizing moments is all about:

> I have a great friend down in Montgomery, Alabama, and a few years ago he told me an unforgettable story of a summer vacation he had planned

for his wife and children. He was unable to go himself because of business, but he helped them plan every day of a camping trip in the family station wagon from Montgomery all the way to California, up and down the West Coast, and then back to Montgomery.

He knew their route exactly and the precise time they would be crossing the Great Divide. So, my friend arranged to fly himself out to the nearest airport and hire a car and a driver to take him to a place which every car must pass. He sat by the side of the road for several hours waiting for the sight of that familiar station wagon. When it came into view, he stepped out on the road and put his thumb out to hitchhike a ride with the family who assumed that he was 3000 miles away.

I said to him, "Coleman, I'm surprised they didn't drive off the road in terror or drop dead of a heart attack. What an incredible story. Why did you go to all that trouble?"

"Well, Bruce," he said, "someday I'm going to be dead, and when that happens, I want my kids and my wife to say, 'You know, Dad was a lot of fun.'"

Wow, I thought. Here is a man whose whole game plan is to make fun and happiness for other people.

It made me wonder what my family will remember about me. I'm sure they will say, "Well, Dad was a nice guy but he sure worried a lot about putting out the lights and closing the windows and picking up around the house and cutting the grass." But I'd also like them to be able to say that Dad was the guy who made life a lot of fun.[6]

That's it! I want each of my three kids to be able to say, "Dad made life a lot of fun."

AT SCHOOL

I've had many special moments with my kids at their schools. The flashy events have been field trips, including a couple of overnighters, and field days where I've cheered them on in their various races, contests, and tugs-of-war.

But when I think about the kids' schools, two main images come to mind that are priceless. One is of six-year-old Eric marching into his school dressed like a miniature Moses (including flowing white beard), the character he was portraying on "My Favorite Character from Literature Day." After school, he told us how one of his classmates came up to him and asked, "Are you God?" The other image is really a collage of the beaming faces when Daddy showed up at school in their younger years. I'm glad that they could be proud of their dad for that reason and in that short season of their lives.

BRIEF WORDS THAT WORK WONDERS

I couldn't close a chapter on seizing moments with children without saying something about the power of words. Leading the list are "I love you," especially as the last words they hear before they go to sleep. A powerful two-word phrase is "I'm sorry"— when heard from Dad, it melts hearts and barriers and also builds character in children who will find it easier to say those two words in later years. Other words that take five seconds or less are "Thank you, good job," and "You sure look nice today."

Isn't it wonderful that we can do so much for our kids in such a short space of time!

POINTS TO REMEMBER

- So much of the joy of fathering comes in the little moments tucked into each and every day.
- A hallmark of a dad who can seize many moments with his kids is spontaneity.
- When you become present focused, you can easily see pockets of time with your kids that you can creatively fill.
- When your child asks you to do something when you're tired or grumpy, before saying no or later, look at the child's face for just five seconds.
- Always try to respond to a child's interests, remembering that relationship is more important than smooth gravy.
- I'd like my kids to be able to say that Dad was the one who made life a lot of fun.
- Show up at your child's school and enjoy the beaming face.
- Two- to five-word phrases, such as "I'm sorry" or "Thank you, good job," work wonders in less than one-half minute.

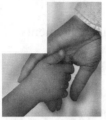

CHAPTER 3

MAKING MEMORIES

What is a family meant to be? Among other things, I personally have always felt it is meant to be a museum of memories—collections of carefully preserved memories.
—EDITH SCHAEFFER

THIS CHAPTER is exclusively a first-person chapter, relying on Hamrin family experiences to illustrate the value and joy of making special memories for your kids. I realize that not every one of these memory-making experiences will appeal to you or apply to your situation. But I am confident that if you put even one into practice, thereby making one new type of special memory for your children, you and your children will be that much richer, and I will feel that my sharing of our family experiences has been well worth it.

The instant I heard the phrase "making a memory" I fell in love with it. It captured me instantly because it expressed so precisely what I have been attempting to do for my kids over the past several years. I have been engaged in making a memory here and making a memory there so that in the end, when they are adults, they will hold a sweet and variegated bouquet of childhood memories.

This notion comes from the sentimental side of me. I had a relatively uncluttered childhood that flowed along quite serenely but was punctuated by those special occasions—those stars on the calendar—that make childhood the enthralling period of life it can, and should, be.

What pops into your mind immediately when the word *childhood* is mentioned? I tried this exercise myself. The first three things that sprang to mind were Christmas Eve, July Fourth picnics, and family vacations (particularly one to Florida). In a second echelon of memories that came along in the next half minute were going to summer camp and eating at Phil Johnson's restaurant after church on Sunday. Finally, the next couple of minutes of deeper mind dredging unearthed Saturday nights at Elsie and Elmer's (when I got to be with my cousin Beverly), Kiddieland and Riverview Amusement Park, baseball games (the Cubs, the White Sox, or the "small time" games at Thillens Stadium), and Sunday school picnics.

Those highlights came to mind in three minutes of reflection. I'm sure the list could be three or even five times longer if I pondered long enough. But I believe that the ones I have listed are the truly special times that helped to define my childhood and give it its zest. I am now trying to pass on this zest for life to my kids.

This primary list of seemingly random, wide-ranging events is quite revealing; it has a common theme. And it is a theme that all these years I have been imparting subconsciously to my kids—childhood memories center on family experiences. I find this fact fascinating, for probably the majority of one's childhood waking hours are spent apart from one's parents—primarily at school, at sports events, and with friends. Yet only going to summer camp and to Riverview (the 1950s Chicago version of Disney World) involved activities just with friends. All the rest involved my parents and me.

Another theme is that *all* of the memories are "going someplace" activities. I'm sure that Carol will get a chuckle from this because she's always teasing me about the Hamrins on the go, how we always want to be doing something and going somewhere. Perhaps for you and your family, the best memories will be quieter, at-home times.

I have devoted so much space to my childhood memories for three reasons: (1) to show the importance of major childhood memories; (2) to show that they will quite likely center on shared family times; and (3) to make the point that if you are interested in the idea of making a memory for your children, go right ahead and draw on your experiences. Virtually everyone has some especially fond memories, and if they delighted you as a youth, they're likely to delight you now. If you're enjoying the activity, it's likely that your kids will enjoy it. Just last week, Carol had the fun of reliving her favorite amusement park ride—the rocko-plane—by introducing it to Eric.

What goes into the process of memory making? Can structure really be given to something that sounds so natural, so free-flowing? I believe that structure can be given to it, and that such structure will benefit the making of memories.

In my case, the structure consists of categories in which special memories are fashioned. All developed naturally and somewhere along the line became "institutionalized" as events that should be kept going and nurtured: annual traditions, family reading times, and times with Grandma and Grandpa.

ANNUAL TRADITIONS

"Tradition, tradition"—I love those big, booming words of Tevye in the musical *Fiddler on the Roof*. I love them because I love traditions. What else so naturally links you with the past while connecting you to the future?

Traditions can come in many shapes, sizes, and time frames.

My favorites are the annual traditions. I'm sure the wellspring for this feeling is the regularity of the Christmas season (and Fourth of July, for that matter, since it was number two on my childhood memory list).

Doing something year after year somehow adds to certainty and security in the midst of a fast-changing world.

HOLIDAYS

What can you do with your kids to make holidays memorable? I would first recommend focusing on religious holidays of importance to your family.

A major tradition—inherited from my older brother's family—is the Sunday evening Advent services. On each of the four Sunday evenings before Christmas, we gather around the Advent wreath in the family room, and we have a short service that Carol tailors to the kids' current age levels—Christmas carols, poems, and verses from the Bible. The services culminate on Christmas Eve when the big center candle is lit. We usually invite friends to join us each Sunday.

Gathering around the glow of the candles from the Advent wreath makes the time festive. Each child has a turn to light a candle each week (and/or blow it out). As is often the case, I doubt if the kids will recall many of the specific words that were said. But the visual image and emotional imprint of sitting in a still candlelit room—while singing Christmas carols and waiting a turn to read a verse or a poem—will not fade. Indeed, those candles may glow even brighter in the mind's eye as they turn nineteen, thirty-nine, and seventy-nine.

Another tradition is choosing and decorating the Christmas tree. When the kids were younger, Carol and I would comb the tree lot for the choicest trees and then hold up two or three for the children to pick from. When they got a bit older, we introduced them to the joy of cutting our own tree. It's always fun to hear the kids render their judgments: "No, the shape's not right" or "This has got to be the one." Interestingly, this is one of the few occasions when consensus among all the children is achieved with remarkable speed and equanimity.

The kids really enjoy decorating the tree. They delight in the ornaments they made as little kids, the wedding ornament (which Mom and Dad hang together with a traditional kiss), and Grandma Lee's fragile glass ornaments. When the tree is fully decorated, all house lights are turned out as we stand around and sing "O Christmas Tree" and take the annual picture of the tree in full dress.

And the evening always ends with Dad's private tradition. After all the work and excitement of decorating the tree, when the kids are in bed, I sit down to enjoy the stillness, the soft glow of the tree lights and, most of all, the memories of Christmas past and the promise of Christmas to come.

Finally, to make Christmas Eve really special, we decided when the kids were young that we would focus on the true meaning of Christmas and ward off the crass commercialism by having a birthday party for Jesus: cake, ice cream, the whole works. And we invite a few of our good friends with kids the same ages as ours to help celebrate.

Thus was born the annual Christmas Eve birthday party at the Hamrins. A few years ago, Carol got the bright idea of having everyone bring a birthday gift. The gift is part of oneself expressed on the piano, violin, cello, recorder, or guitar; it can be a song, a poem, or a humorous skit. We've had them all. The kids love it. The adults love it.

Twenty or thirty years from now, if someone were to ask my kids what they most remember about their childhood holidays, they are quite likely to indicate the Christmas Eve birthday parties with all the songs, laughter, and gaiety.

Most other major holidays have special traditions, too.

On the Fourth of July, when the children were small, we switched from attending the big parade, concert, and fireworks in Washington, D.C., to enjoying local parades, a town barbecue at the village green, and local fireworks. But the last couple of years the kids once again wanted to see the big ones in D.C.

On Easter, after sunrise service at a nearby lake, the kids enjoy an early morning jelly bean hunt with the usual "impossible to find" ones carefully placed by Dad.

On Labor Day, we go on a midmorning breakfast picnic with about thirty friends and friends of friends. A spirited volleyball game, kids included, always works off the breakfast.

We usually spend Thanksgiving at the Bernbaums' house, with John and Marge, the seven kids in their household, usually at least one grandmother, and often a few college kids away from home. Lots of people gathered around a table—that's my idea of a good Thanksgiving. It's one of those times of the year when we all get around to serious game playing: football, basketball, Ping-Pong, pool, and numerous board games.

BIRTHDAYS

The way I look at it, kids really get into and remember birthday parties, particularly from ages five to eleven. That's seven parties, few enough that parents can really work to make them something special. (By the way, showing a video is not something special in my book.)

To ensure that they're special, ask your children what they want to do. Assuming that they don't ask to go off to Disney World with a half dozen friends, try to deliver. And dads, try to be there. I believe I've been at every one of my three children's parties. And without exception, I've had a great time. You may ask,

"What does a dad do at a birthday party?"

Your role might be quite different for boys' or girls' parties. Eric wanted games that centered on athletic contests. So I stage-managed a Junior Olympics with ten events and points awarded to the top five finishers in each event: 10, 7, 5, 3, and 1. Awarding points to the top five when there are only eight to ten boys assures that each boy will get a goodly number of points.

At Krista and Kira's birthday parties, I play more of a supporting role, including the filming. The most enjoyable moment of these parties is observing arrival time: after the first girl arrives, all three run up the driveway to greet the next arrival (well before she disembarks from the car), then back to the house, only to run back up again, squealing and shouting as the next car appears around the corner, ad infinitum until the fifteenth girl finally arrives amidst a cacophony of screeches and swirling bodies. No rock star has ever received a more frenzied, tumultuous welcome.

Many of their parties inevitably take place on a weekday. That's a fringe benefit that comes from being your own boss. But I would urge any dad with a boss to plan ahead to take a few hours off once or twice a year. Remember, there are only about seven memorable birthday parties for each child. And for the child, each one will be an extra-special memory with Dad in the picture.

In recent years, we have added another birthday tradition the kids really love—breakfast in bed. The special birthday honoree (child or parent) sits in bed and waits for a favorite breakfast to be brought in. After the breakfast is finished, the cards and presents are opened. It's a wonderful follow-on for kids who have outgrown birthday parties.

SPECIAL EVENTS

Other traditions revolve around what we refer to as special events. It began several years ago with the Scottish Christmas Walk, a short parade that occurs on the first Saturday of

December each year down the streets of Old Town Alexandria. It's full of bagpipers, wolfhounds, Saint. Bernards, Scotties, antique cars, and marching Scottish clans. Carol and I began going to it well before we had kids, and we just took them along as they arrived on the scene. Both Carol and I like returning to the same event each year—same time, same place on the sidewalk. This day, along with our first Advent service, marks the opening of the Christmas season for us.

I noticed sometime in the early 1980s that we were attending other events that the whole family enjoyed. Rather than take a chance of forgetting them, I decided to put them on the calendar at the first of the year. It's not a dramatic idea but one that works. I've been amazed at the number of my friends who say, "Oh, I forgot about that," when it's a regular monthly or yearly event; there are power and sanity in a single organizing calendar on which you put all family member activities to avoid lapses or conflicts.

So now, as each new year's calendar arrives, I turn first to April and mark the second Saturday for our annual bluebell walk along Bull Run—our family's way of greeting spring each year. Next, I turn to the last weekend of May and mark in Cedar Point Farm, a lovely spot on the eastern shore of the Chesapeake Bay, where Carol and I head for some spiritual nourishment (at the C. S. Lewis Institute's annual Memorial Day weekend seminar) while the kids explore the waterfront for crabs, oysters, and all sorts of mysterious (and sometimes smelly) treasures.

The fall season is marked by two extra-special special events. The Bluemont Fair is held the third weekend in September. Formerly known as Snickersville, Bluemont is a tiny hamlet nestled into the foothills of the Shenandoah Mountains in the northwestern corner of Virginia. The drive through the gently rolling horse country, mostly on back roads, is half the fun of the day. For a weekend, the whole town of Bluemont is transformed into a turn-of-the-century-style fair: bluegrass singing, banjo playing, clogging, crafts, barbecue chicken, antiques, kids' games, animals to pet. Straight out of a Norman Rockwell painting.

As far as I'm concerned, the more Norman Rockwell paintings we engrave in our children's minds, the better. Simple, inexpensive, down-home fun is what it is all about.

The October special event has become the family favorite. Four years ago, we booked a rustic cabin at Cacapon State Park in the West Virginia panhandle, only about two hours away. The cabin was ideal—two giant rooms divided by a huge stone fireplace with lofts for sleeping at the end of each room. We roast marshmallows to make s'mores (graham cracker, chocolate square, and marshmallow sandwiches) on Saturday evening; we hike, see deer everywhere, and eat delicious, inexpensive meals at the lodge.

The kids so reveled in the rustic beauty of the cabin and the state park setting the first time that we immediately decided to add the stay to our special events list. Again, it does not just happen. Indeed, it takes long-range planning. Precisely at 8:00 A.M. on October 1, I must call the state park to book the cabin for the following October. Thus, October 1 is marked on the calendar each year as well. It's not quite the same as having a cabin of our own, but returning to the same cabin each year provides a memory of autumns spent at the cabin that our kids will long cherish.

December brings the year's final annual event; the weekend following the Scottish Christmas Walk, we give our kids a taste of their Scandinavian heritage by going to the Santa Lucia Festival. Who could forget the sights and sounds of the Lucia procession as the Lucia girl, bedecked with a wreath of candles on her head, leads a group of children down the aisle to the melodious sounds of "Santa Lucia" in an otherwise hushed and darkened church?

For everyone, candles leave an indelible impression on the mind's—and soul's—eye.

FAMILY READING TIMES

Now we switch gears. Most of the annual traditions described so far involved motion—going someplace.

Another type of memory is equally important to give to your children—quiet times. Our family loves to sit on the deck watching summer's fireflies, autumn's sunsets, and winter's quiet snowfalls. And there's no better quiet time than family reading.

I must make a confession. We have not been as successful in this arena as we have been in the more active fun times. In part, since I enjoy "doing" so much, and young kids do, too, we're more naturally inclined to follow that route. But I do enjoy reading, my wife positively loves reading, and all of us have enjoyed tremendously our family reading times.

The key is discipline. Virtually all of the other memory makers described in this chapter are events that can be put on the calendar, and when the time comes, we do them. So, too, with family reading time. A catch-as-catch-can approach doesn't work—the "can" part never materializes. This approach falls victim to sheer forgetfulness or competing, more exciting, alternatives. We have used instead a daily or a weekly exercise in which we read through a book for a week or maybe a month, or a longer book or series of books weekly for a few months.

The biggest success by far was our first effort: we read the *Chronicles of Narnia* series by C. S. Lewis. Carol had read the seven books as a young adult. She loved them. I had heard enough snatches from them as well as testimonies from others about the delightful times they had had reading them with their kids that I was primed to go. In fact, I had to restrain myself for about two years to give my daughters time to "mature" to the right age (six to eight) to really enjoy the series.

So Carol and I announced in October 1986 that the time had arrived when the wonderful family adventure of living in Narnia for a few weeks was about to begin. Every night, right after supper, we gathered in the family room to journey to Narnia. Krista and Kira snuggled up on either side of the reader on the big sofa, and Eric curled up with the other parent on the loveseat. The sheer feeling of togetherness as a family was an extra-special benefit of the times together.

Carol and I would take turns reading the books. I was so glad that I started, for that meant I got to read four. Honestly, I would have loved to read all seven, but I knew I had to share the delight with Carol.

Let me tell you what's on my mind right now as I write this section. I have the almost overpowering urge to start reading through the whole series again—tonight! And I realize that reading the *Chronicles of Narnia* together, along with Christmas mornings and a special family vacation or two, is going to be one of my most precious memories of our children's younger days.

That's quite revealing to me, for it highlights how much I, Carol, and the kids missed out by not having this as a higher priority all along. We have made a mistake here.

Family reading time can also build a sense of family identity, roots, and pride.

When the kids were ages seven and ten, we took a car trip to South Dakota to trace the trail Carol's ancestors had taken through Wisconsin and Minnesota on their way to South Dakota after coming from Norway via the Great Lakes in 1854. The migration trail was remarkably similar to that taken by the Ingalls family in the Laura Ingalls Wilder series of books. So we read several of these books in the van as we traveled through the exact places we were reading about and where Carol's ancestors had gone at approximately the same time as the Ingalls. The whole trip, with the readings, unexpectedly helped Eric to bond with South Dakota.

There come times when the content of family night has to change to suit changing family dynamics. Somewhere in the teen years, that line is easily crossed when family reading time seems a bore, and the magic of places like Narnia is thought to be only for "little kids" (and, of course, their parents). I am reminded of the time in the famous song "Puff" when the little boy Jackie came no more and Puff the Magic Dragon ceased his fearless roar. That imagery always bothered me as my kids were approaching their adolescent years.

I know—intellectually—that to cope with the harsh realities of the world, each person must shed childhood innocence. I know that. But it doesn't mean I have to like it when it comes to my kids.

So I want to soak in all the snuggles I can get from my children, for snuggling time also soon passes. And I want to hear once again the excited chorus of three voices saying, "Don't stop there. We can't stop there. Just one more chapter, Daddy. PLEASE!"

TIMES WITH GRANDMA AND GRANDPA

Up to this point, we've been talking about making memories with the immediate family. Left out of the picture thus far have been Grandma and Grandpa—two rather significant people in the whole scheme of things.

Yet too often in today's society, Grandma and Grandpa are too easily forgotten. Not forgotten in the literal sense of out of sight, out of mind, but in the practical sense of being an active, vital part of the lives of their grandchildren. Many families live far apart. Some grandparents would like to be with their grandchildren more often, but they don't want to intrude, don't want to appear too pushy. Other grandparents are too busy to make room in their schedules for their grandchildren. Much of this book could be creatively applied by a granddad; it's never too late to start on great grandfathering.

So, it's time to take the initiative. How? What are the ways that kids can get to know, enjoy, and benefit from their grandparents?

First, foremost, and last, *they have to be with them*. Remember the title of this part of the book—"Being There." There is no substitute for getting them together. And that means inviting them to your house, taking your family to their house, sending one (or some combination) of the kids to Grandma and Grandpa's house, or meeting them somewhere on vacation. A mixture of all four over the course of your children's childhoods would be ideal.

Managing these get-togethers will involve some sacrifice. For the past several years, when my parents were too ill to travel, we have driven fifteen hundred miles to Chicago and back to be with them, giving up alternative, more exciting, or relaxing vacation plans. But the issue always comes down to what is really important.

In practice, the number one option will likely be to have grandparents visit your house, especially when your kids are at an age requiring childproof decor. And grandparents can relax and enjoy them more if they are guests, not hosts.

Grandparents can be fun. Some of the most fun-filled times my children have had have been with their grandparents. My most vivid memory of Grandma Lee (Carol's mom) was at Wild World, a midsized amusement park just a few miles outside the beltway in Maryland. She was around sixty-three; she had cancer. Yet there she was, climbing up the long flight of stairs to the twisting water slides and sloshing down with one of her granddaughters in her lap—repeatedly. But it was the pirate ship ride that I most remember. It rocks back and forth, higher and higher, until you're fifty feet up and looking almost straight down.

Well, I couldn't get Carol to go with me. Nor could I get my daughters. Not even my six-year-old son. But Grandma Lee was ready for it. Carol and I gave each other a "should we really let her do it?" look, shrugged, and I said, "Let's go."

The ride was even rougher and scarier than I had expected. I was a bit concerned about her and hoped that we hadn't ruined an otherwise great day. When we got off, I asked her, "Well, what do you think?"

"It was great."

"Like to go again?" I asked jokingly.

"Sure."

I said, "You've got to be kidding!" She wasn't. We went again. She loved it again. Wish I could say the same.

Her keen appreciation of every aspect of life—from going on exciting outings to quietly gathering wildflower bouquets (before they were "in")—is a memory of her the children and I will always treasure.

Grandma and Grandpa Hamrin also always had a zest for life. They loved to do things. To go places. To be with people.

Whenever they visited us, we made it a big deal. All five of us turned out to meet them at the airport—right at the end of the gate. And that's been true whether it's a 2:00 P.M. arrival (haul the kids out of school) or a 12:15 A.M. arrival (haul the kids out of bed). You see, hard as it is to believe, I think that kids still find trips to the airport exciting and therefore memorable. (I only wish I could forget most of my recent ones.)

While they are here, we often live the Hamrin tradition with three generations—going to a lot of places. Only in their late seventies did they finally slow down. But that hasn't stopped Mom from getting down on the floor to play with her grandchildren. And it certainly didn't stop both of them from playing board and card games with the kids.

Aside from these ordinary visits, we have given our kids two special times with Grandma and Grandpa. In February 1987, we arranged for my parents during their visit to the south to meet us for a few days on our first trip to Disney World. Sharing that delightful place with Grandma and Grandpa turned a fun trip into an extra-special trip.

The other time they really got a good chance to get to know one another was only four months later when we flew my parents here to stay with our kids while we had a second honeymoon. For two full weeks, they played, they read, and they laughed together. And they went off to the emergency room after Krista broke her wrist—the one type of thing they were fearing might happen did happen. But despite that, the reports from all parties were glowing when we got back.

POINTS TO REMEMBER
- Main childhood memories center on family experiences.
- In making a memory for your children, feel free to draw on your childhood experiences.
- Possible structures under which special memories can be fashioned are annual traditions, family reading times, and times with Grandma and Grandpa.
- Holiday traditions can include lighting candles and holding weekly services. Encourage participation by the kids as much as possible.
- Because kids really "get into" and remember birthday parties, try to make them something special. Most important, be there.
- Breakfast in bed on one's birthday can be a delightful yearly tradition for a child.
- Look for annual special events that the kids enjoy going to, and put them on your calendar early in the year.
- Family reading time can provide some of the most special memories.
- Take the initiative in encouraging Grandma and Grandpa to be an active, vital part of the lives of their grandchildren.
- Remember, grandparents can be fun.

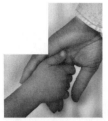

CHAPTER 4

ENJOYING THE BABY

The way for a father to become companionable with his children is to participate fully in the care of his first baby from the day she comes home and to keep on participating.
—DR. BENJAMIN SPOCK

IT IS ONE of those perfect June days. The sky is a rich luminescent blue; the sun is warm; the air is crisp. June 19, 1977—Father's Day. And I am bringing home my new baby—my son Eric—from the hospital. It doesn't come any better than this, a thrill beyond any I have previously experienced.

Two weeks later, I'm pacing the living room floor with Eric in his Snuggly on my chest. He's wailing at the top of his little lungs as he has been for twenty minutes straight. With rising agitation, I stride out the front door and down the street, exhorting him ever more loudly: "Just keep quiet. Settle down. What's the matter with you anyway?" I feel in my complete frustration that I'm about to explode, an agony unlike any I have ever experienced.

THE THRILL OF VICTORY—THE AGONY OF DEFEAT

"The thrill of victory—the agony of defeat." I can think of no better summary of what being with a baby is all about. In fact, I'd go so far as to say that this "Wide World of Sports" expression is stated more perfectly each week in and week out by the parent of a new baby than by any athlete in any sporting event.

So if you're the father of a baby, or you will be the father of a baby in the near future, theme number one to remember is that there will be both the thrill of victory and the agony of defeat. The whole experience, particularly the first few weeks but throughout the baby's first year, can be an emotional roller-coaster ride. In her book *The Birth of a Father*, Cecilia Worth acknowledges the wide range of responses and emotions that men can experience as the father of a baby: the isolation, the anger, the distancing, the excitement, the wonder, and the nurturing. I'm also reminded of the three *E*'s of Robert Samuelson, one of my favorite columnists who writes for *Newsweek*: "My children are exasperating, exhausting, and exhilarating. They are the best part of me, and I won't miss their growing up."

That's the spirit I hope you have as the father of a baby. It's what I had from day one, and I've never regretted it, even with all the exasperating and exhausting times involved. Let's take a closer look at the types of thrills and agonies that are in store for you or relive the types you've already had.

The thrills that come with being a new father begin even before the birth. Encompassed are those tender moments that you and your wife share as you observe and discuss the miracle that is happening inside her—the thought that your child is forming. The first kick she feels. Hearing the heartbeat. The excitement and trepidation of each day when "it could happen any moment."

Then the big day arrives. You coach and encourage your wife through labor the best you know how, then rush excitedly into the blur of the delivery room. And finally the mystical, magical moment arrives: the tiny and fragile new human being is placed into your arms for the first time. "This is it. It's real. This baby is mine." It's quite a rush, quite a thrill!

So what lies ahead?

If you adopt the right attitude—the attitude that babies can be fun—you'll soon discover just how much fun they can be.

You'll laugh like you haven't laughed in years at the antics, the quirks, the constant surprises. But the key word is *attitude*. You've got to release yourself to have fun, to drop the mask, to check the dignified persona at the door. I like the way Jim Sanderson talks of dads "coming out of their dignity" and "allowing themselves to suspend judgment for a few moments as to what is real and useful." In a world where so much is serious, wouldn't it be sheer pleasure to have lots of moments to come out of our dignity?

Another unexpected thrill was taking Eric anywhere we wanted to. After eight years of marriage with no kids and a decent income, we had become rather spoiled in a lifestyle of freedom. I logically drew the conclusion that all that would come to a crashing halt following Eric's arrival.

What a pleasant surprise to discover that Eric could accompany us. We took off for Aspen, Colorado, for a two-week conference when he was two weeks old. Virtually every one of those fourteen nights we went to a different restaurant for dinner, and there was tiny Eric asleep beside us. Traveling with him continued throughout his first two years, culminating in a round-the-world trip with a four-month stay in China as he turned two. We had a terrific time as our towhead quickly became a "star" in China where most of the people we met had never seen a fair-haired child before. We returned to the States that fall; Eric was twenty-eight months old, and he had completed his fifty-sixth airplane flight—vivid testimony to the fact that a baby does not have to restrict or confine you in any fundamental way if you're willing to be a bit adventuresome.

All right, let's do our reality check and turn to the agony of defeat to get the whole picture in tending to baby.

I've already shared one agony—Eric's crying fits for twenty to thirty nonstop minutes. Frustration. Anger. And finally guilt for having such feelings when we found out that he was crying because he was not getting enough breast milk. A transfer to formula brought an instant end to the crying bouts.

Another type of agony that I'm sure many dads suffer is moments of panic. One such experience was when eighteen-month-old Eric wandered from the house. I was taking out the garbage and left the front door open briefly. Well, briefly is all an eighteen-month-old needs. He was gone in a flash. Not knowing where he was at first, I calmly looked all around the house, calling out his name. My pace then quickened as I walked all around the outside of our house, yelling out his name. When he was nowhere in sight, panic set in as I raced down the streets of our neighborhood, screaming out his name. Of course, the worst scenarios were popping into my mind. He must have gone into the creek or down the sewer drain opening in front of our house.

There's no panic quite like what sets in when you feel your baby—in this case our one and only baby—is in serious jeopardy. There's also no feeling of relief quite like what you feel as a father after a forty-five minute panic attack and you see your baby safely arriving home in the lap of a neighbor (who had driven blocks away and found Eric peacefully ambling down the center of the street).

Another panic attack occurred when Kira was one. She was in the midst of an infrequent, but very intense, crying bout (we have subsequently seen that it was just an early manifestation of her tendency to do everything with gusto) when she went rigid, rolled her eyes up, and collapsed on the floor. I thought it was all over. I mean it was red alert! I can't even remember exactly what I did other than shake her and offer a very quick prayer for God to please revive her. Fortunately, the rigor mortis lasted "only" about twenty to twenty-five seconds. But those were seconds of sheer agony. Only later, in calm and rational moments, did I learn that such frightening states are caused by temporary lack of oxygen from the intense crying.

An agony that I suffered, and I believe is quite prevalent among many couples, was guilt over sending a baby to day care. In 1977 and 1978, Carol and I were really into our careers in Washington, we loved our jobs, and the jobs paid well. I remember reasoning at the time: it would be silly to give up a good-paying job if we could get (as we did) good day care for a reasonable cost. As an efficient economist, I saw a positive benefit-cost ratio to having Eric in day care. Besides, we worked around the margins to limit the time he was in day care through flexible working hours and my working at home on Thursdays. It wasn't until the girls arrived that it began to really hit me: "Hey, I have three wonderful children, two of whom are just babies and need our love and hugs more than anything right now. No more full-time, or even close to full-time day care."

Anger. Panic. Guilt. These are the main ways I experienced the agony of defeat in the babyhood years of our children. But I tell you the truth—I wouldn't trade those years for anything. The experiences taught me a lot—particularly patience, which was not my strong suit before the children arrived. I also learned invaluable lessons in being flexible, having a sense of humor, and making instant decisions that served me well throughout my children's developmental years.

So if you're just starting out with a new baby under your roof or one is on the way, keep in mind that all first-time dads enter the experience with one thing in common: no track record and usually little training. But most work their way through it pretty well and actually emerge from the process as a better father (and often a better man).

The story is told of the young vice president who came in to see the crusty president who was retiring. He asked the older gent his secret of success.

> The president replied, "Young man, two words: good decisions!"
>
> "Thank you very much, sir. But how does one make good decisions?" the young vice president wanted to know.
>
> "One word, young man: experience!"
>
> "Yes sir, but how does one get experience?"
>
> "Two words, young man: bad decisions!"[1]

NO LIMIT TO LOVE

Theme number two to remember is love. Not much more needs to be said than babies cannot get too much love. They thrive on it.

Do you want your baby to get off to a great start in life? Love him. Love her. Hold the baby a lot. Play. Laugh. Smile. Spell love T-I-M-E.

I can't remember exactly how many months old he was, but Eric (and later Kira and Krista) began to hear very early on "I love you" from Dad every night just before going to sleep.

BE A NURTURING DAD

The third theme is nurture. Be a nurturing dad. Look forward to providing moments of tender loving care to your baby. Don't leave hugs and snuggling to Mom.

But nurturing involves far more than TLC. It's a very rich concept that according to *Webster's* means "to raise or promote the development of; to educate; to bring up or train up." Defined properly, it seems obvious that every dad should be a nurturing dad.

Just how important and exciting is the challenge to us dads of nurturing each child? Dr. Albert Siegel has observed, "When it comes to rearing children, every society is only twenty years from barbarism. Twenty years is all we have to accomplish the task of civilizing the infants who are born into our midst each year."[2]

Fine. It's important. But doesn't a baby naturally gravitate to Mom as the primary nurturer? I held this assumption as I started on the venture of fathering. Since then, I've learned from experience and from studies that it just isn't so. A number of studies have shown that by the age of twenty months, children are as attached to their fathers as to their mothers. And here's a bit of encouraging news: children actually prefer Dad over Mom during playtime. Children of both sexes were more involved, cooperative, excited, and interested when playing with their fathers than with their mothers. Children want us dads to be involved in their lives, whether it's at age sixteen months or sixteen years.

"Okay," you say. "Sounds great. I want to be a nurturing dad. Where do I start? What's involved? Are other nurturing dads out there? What are they like?"

Fortunately, one source provides answers to all these questions. It is *The Nurturing Father* by Dr. Kyle Pruett, a clinical professor of psychiatry at the Yale University Child Study Center.[3] If you really want all the details, you can read through the whole book. But for those without such time and energy, I'll summarize his key findings and suggestions.

Dr. Pruett says, "We begin where a man needs to start thinking of himself as a father"—during pregnancy. Help choose the obstetrician or health care system for the mother's prenatal care. Share daydreams and naming games for your future child so that bonding in your heart and mind can begin. Some of our younger friends are having baby showers that include Dad as well as Mom.

Play an active role in the birthing process.

A helpful insight from Dr. Pruett is that while men can and do nurture, interact with, and competently rear children, they do these things *differently* from women. Not worse, not better—just differently. Thus, the more accurate universal truth is not "Father Knows Best" but "Father Knows Differently."

What are nurturing dads like? In looking for consistent factors among nurturing dads, Dr. Pruett could identify few. But he did find a "pervasive, involving, committed fatherliness about these men." In short, it's primarily a matter of attitude and will.

Any man can become a nurturing father.

Dr. Pruett shared that a nurturing dad understood and welcomed the child's ability and power to affect his life, and developed his own ability to allow his life to be affected by his child. Pruett stated, "This power to influence each other's lives is the news this book has to tell." This is really an exciting thought, for it shows the real wellspring of many nurturing dads: the baby. The baby makes an enormous contribution to the development of a nurturing dad by evoking, provoking, eliciting, promoting, and nudging fathering from a man.

So watch out, new dad—you may become a nurturing dad when you least expect it. Allow it to happen. Be open to it. Don't resist. Dr. Pruett concludes his book with what he terms the heart of its message, which "is not that all men need to rear their children full time in order to become truly nurturing human beings, but that men must shape, and be allowed to shape, their lives so that they may discover and develop their own full creative talents as nurturing men."

When you're open, remarkable things can happen from the subtle nudging of a baby. Witness this transformation in the life of a twenty-two-year-old affluent computer-wizard first-time father, who was at the hospital after his six-month-old son recovered from a life-threatening respiratory illness:

> Things will never be the same again for me. I used to think, "With my brains and money nothing could touch me"—and I thought it was supposed to be like that. I don't even think I could cry. Now I am worried that I feel too much—you know—can't get it back together? But I will, I always do. I hope I don't forget, though. I feel like I know my son so well now. I took every breath with him for four days and nights.[4]

I've always viewed the fathering process as analogous to the efforts of a gardener. A good gardener is very concerned about his plants. He knows what each one needs. He knows how to properly prepare the soil—the plants' surrounding environment. He knows when and how much to water them. He knows when to prune them. He keeps the weeds and bugs away. His overall objective is the plant's healthy growth into a thing of beauty.

POINTS TO REMEMBER

- "The thrill of victory—the agony of defeat"—there is no better summary of what being with a baby is all about.
- If you adopt the right attitude—the attitude that babies can be fun—you'll soon discover just how much fun they can be.
- Come out of your dignity and allow yourself to suspend judgment for a few moments about what is real and useful.
- A baby does not have to restrict or confine you in any fundamental way if you're willing to be a bit adventuresome.
- Anger. Panic. Guilt. These are some of the main ways you may experience the agony of defeat in the babyhood years of

your children.

- Babies cannot get too much love. They thrive on it.
- By the age of twenty months, children are as attached to their fathers as to their mothers, and young children actually prefer Dad over Mom during playtime.
- Nurturing dads display a "pervasive, involving, committed fatherliness."
- The baby makes an enormous contribution to the development of a nurturing dad by evoking, provoking, eliciting, promoting, and nudging fathering from a man.
- As a gardener carefully tends his plants so they can grow healthy and to full maturity and beauty, so a father should tend his children.

CHAPTER 5

FILLING THE EMOTIONAL TANKS OF TEENAGERS

When I was a boy of 14, my father was so ignorant I could hardly stand to have the Old Man around. But when I got to be 21, I was astonished at how much he had learned in seven years.
—MARK TWAIN

OR TO phrase it differently, *don't count the score at halftime.* That's probably the most hopeful, and perhaps helpful, sentence in this entire book. If only we dads could really believe it in our heart of hearts and live by that motto.

The teenage years. The very phrase almost automatically strikes terror in your heart after hearing and reading all the horror stories about this crazy, mixed-up time. You're likely to suffer some stress and agony as each of your children marches through those years of thirteen to nineteen. And along the way, at some point you're going to say "amen" to another Mark Twain aphorism, this one on how to rear a teenager:

Things run along pretty smoothly until your kid reaches thirteen. That's the time you need to stick him in a barrel, hammer the lid down nice and snug, and feed him through the knot-hole. And then, about the time he turns sixteen, plug up the knot-hole.

James Dobson draws a wonderful analogy between adolescents and the very early space probes that blasted off from Cape Canaveral in Florida. I call it the blast-off, reentry analogy. I share it with you not only for its good humor (which we need above all else when parenting teens) but for its illustration of the universality of the adolescent years, what they're all about, and how parents will survive them:

> After the training and preparation of childhood are over, a pubescent youngster marches out to the launching pad. His parents watch apprehensively as he climbs aboard a capsule called adolescence and waits for his rockets to fire. His father and mother wish they could go with him, but there is room for just one person in the spacecraft. Besides, nobody invited them. Without warning, the mighty rocket engines begin to roar and the "umbilical cord" falls away. "Liftoff! We have liftoff!" screams the boy's father.
>
> Junior, who was a baby only yesterday, is on his way to the edge of the universe. A few weeks later, his parents go through the scariest experience of their lives. "Negative ions" have interfered with communication at a time when they most want to be assured of their son's safety. Why won't he talk to them?

This period of silence does not last a few minutes, as it did with Colonel Glenn and friends. It may continue for years. The same kid who used to talk a mile a minute and ask a million questions has now reduced his vocabulary to nine monosyllabic phrases. They are, "I dunno," "Maybe," "I forget," "Huh?" "No!," "Nope," "Yeah," "Who—me?" and "He did it." Otherwise, only "static" comes through the receivers—groans, grunts, growls and gripes. What an apprehensive time it is for those who wait on the ground!

Years later when Mission Control believes the spacecraft to have been lost, a few scratchy signals are picked up unexpectedly from a distant transmitter. The parents are jubilant as they hover near their radio. Was that really his voice? It is deeper and more mature than they remembered. There it is again. This time the intent is unmistakable. Their spacey son has made a deliberate effort to correspond with them! He was fourteen years old when he blasted into space and now he is nearly twenty. Could it be that negative environment has been swept away and communication is again possible? Yes. For most families, that is precisely what happens. After years of quiet anxiety, parents learn to their great relief that everything is A-Okay on board the spacecraft. The "splashdown" occurring during the early twenties can then be a wonderful time of life for both generations.[1]

What are the kids doing while they're "in orbit" and out of touch? A dad needs to understand just what his teens are going through; from such understanding should come greater patience and commitment on his part to do what is necessary to get them (and him) through these tortuous and confusing years.

Confusion. That's a trademark of the teen years. Trapped between childhood and adulthood—not being fully comfortable with either—teens are confused about their identity and self-image, their sexuality, and their values. They are confused about what the future holds and thus sometimes act like children. This mass confusion leads to strong emotions of anger, hostility, withdrawal, and overall frustration. They then release these emotions on the objects most conveniently available and supposedly ones that won't strike back—their parents.

Is this fair? No. But as I keep telling my kids, "Life's not fair." So as dads, we're called upon to bear our unfair share (and help our wives bear theirs) at critical times during our children's teenage years. There's no getting around it, fellow dads, we have to pay the price! But remember, our parents had to pay the price, and theirs did, too. Conflict between parents and their teenage children is one of the given facts of recorded history.

And it's tough because usually we are parenting teens just as we are entering middle age (in our late thirties and forties) and quite possibly a midlife crisis—adult adolescence since it is a time of redefining many areas in our lives, sometimes even a new philosophy of life.

But whatever price we pay as dads is well worth it.

The stakes are simply too high not to pay the necessary price. I'm thinking of the haunting statement, "Highschool girls are the loneliest people in America," and realizing that highschool boys can't be too far behind. I'm thinking about the recent record rate of teen suicide—the tremendously disturbing fact that eight of one hundred teens tried to kill themselves in one year in a county in Michigan. And finally, I'm thinking of the response to the question, "What message would you like to give your parents?" The teen said, "We're not faking it. We need help."

"We need help." What more do we need to hear to make the commitment to pay the necessary price?

OUR ESSENTIAL TASK

How do we respond to this call for help? Out of all the hundreds of pages of material I've read about dealing as a parent with teenagers, one thought stands out. The advice from Dr. Ross Campbell is this: "Only if the emotional tank is full can a teenager be expected to be his best and do his best."[2] Dr. Campbell goes on to explain why refilling a teen's emotional tank is so essential:

> The child must repeatedly return to the parent to have his emotional tank refilled in order to continue his quest for independence. This is exactly what happens with the teenager, especially the early adolescent. He may use different means of exerting his drive for independence (and sometimes in disturbing or upsetting ways). He needs the energy from his emotional tank to do this. And where does he get his emotional tank refilled? Right! From his parents. A teenager will strive for independence in typical adolescent ways—doing things by himself, going places without family, testing parental rules. But he will eventually run out of emotional gasoline and come back to the parent for emotional maintenance—for a refill. This is what we want, as parents of teenagers. We want our adolescent to be able to come to us for emotional maintenance when he needs it.[3]

The fuller the tank, the more positive the feelings, the better the behavior. Be there for the refills.

WHAT TEENS SAY THEY NEED FROM PARENTS

I think we should go to the real experts: teenagers. What do they say they need from their parents? If this method seems a bit risky, rest assured that what teens say usually correlates with the views of parents and experts who deal with adolescents and teens. One major survey of teens concluded with an opportunity for them to offer advice to adults. Here is a summary of the most frequently given advice:

> Try to understand us. Listen when we talk and try to communicate with us. Give us more freedom. Trust us, respect us; don't assume all teen-agers are bad. Set limits and discipline us fairly when we disobey. Show love constantly and consistently. Don't preach at us—it only turns us off. Give encouragement and affirmation when we do things right. Don't condemn us and make us feel guilty. Spend time with us. Pray for us and with us. Be good examples for us. Lead (don't push) us in the right way. Don't yell and make threats, it only causes rebellion. Explain things so we don't get curious and find out in other ways.[4]

Going to the source yielded five clear-cut needs that teens are looking to their parents to fill: (1) love, affection, and a happy home life; (2) rules/boundaries; (3) independence/being trusted; (4) patience and understanding; and (5) affirmation. As we look at ways to meet each of these needs, remember that undergirding all our efforts as dads is the need for wisdom.

> **Wisdom helps us know when it is time to confront or hug, talk or act, listen or affirm.**

Ask God for the wisdom to respond as you should to your teenage child or perhaps to back off and let Him take charge.

1. LOVE, AFFECTION, AND A HAPPY HOME LIFE

What do adolescents and teens want most? What are they really looking for behind their rebellion, anger, or sullenness? It's really basic. They want love. And they want a happy home life.

These fundamental desires are singled out by numerous professionals who work with youths. I put the most confidence in Josh McDowell, who speaks before hundreds of thousands of teens every year and speaks personally with hundreds. Here's how he summarizes all his years of experience:

> But from what I see as I travel a hundred and fifty thousand miles a year talking to high schoolers and collegians, what they are really looking for is leadership, character, integrity, and above all, love.
>
> Do you know what today's lower-age teens (13–15 years) really want? Their number one desire is for a happy home life.... More emphasis on closer family ties is desired by 86 percent of teens, with only slightly greater emphasis on this value noted among young women (90 percent) than among young men (82 percent).... A research institute study showed that out of a list of twenty-four values, the two most important to young adolescents in grades five through nine are "to have a happy home life" and "to get a good job when I am older."[5]

Love. That's good to hear, for of course parents love their kids. But wait. Josh McDowell also points out a very disturbing finding from a survey of several thousand highschool students who were asked what single question they would like their parents to answer: 50 percent said they wanted to know *if their parents loved them.*

I try to demonstrate my love for my kids in numerous ways. It's an area that I've worked hard at. From day one of their lives, I wanted my children to know beyond a shadow of a doubt that their dad loves them dearly. That is why the last words they hear from me each night are "I love you."

And guess what? It works! They let me know that they are assured of my love for them. My daughter Kira expressed it as follows:

> **My dad passed down his love for adventure to me. He gave me joy in my life. That's what I needed, joy. I needed love. He gave that to me also. Never once did a day pass without him saying, "I love you." And my dad always made sure I knew how much he loved me.**

Contrast those feelings with these feelings of a teenage girl:

> **When I was eight years old I first had sex with a boy of fifteen. I did it because I lack love and attention from my parents. I need love, and my parents never show me any. Nothing really changed at home, and at fifteen I became pregnant. My boyfriend blamed me and left. I had nowhere to turn, I was trapped, so I had an abortion. Now I'm afraid to date anyone, and I cry myself to sleep every night.**[6]

So love your teens. Express your love. Show it by hugging them, by spending time with them, by listening to them.

And then provide a happy home life. This idea goes back to many of the suggestions presented earlier about ways to have fun together as a family and to make memories It is based on a happy—that is, a solid, stable, affectionate, fun-loving—relation-ship with your wife. A happy home life is not possible for children who see their parents not getting along.

Just living in a loving environment goes a long way in produc-ing the character building and values formation that you would like to see in your kids. According to one adolescent-parent study,

> adolescents in a close family are the ones most likely to say no to drug use, premarital sexual activity, and other antisocial and alienating behaviors. They are also the ones most likely to adopt high moral standards, develop the ability to make and keep friends, embrace a religious faith, and involve themselves in helping activities. All of these characteristics pertaining to adolescents from close families are significant—which means that the evidence cannot be attributed to mere chance.[7]

Recent studies indicate that teens are shaped more by their par-ents than by their peers that they adopt their parents' values and opinions to a greater extent than anyone realized.

The question that pops up at this point is, But what about my children's friends? And other strong societal influences? No doubt about it—peer pressure, television, movies, and rock music can have a major impact on teens. But the good news is that home is still the most powerful in determining how happy, secure, and stable teenagers are. Teens understand this. That's why the need for love is noted in every survey.

Remember the statement earlier in the chapter, "High school girls are the loneliest people in America"? We dads can do a lot to relieve that loneliness. One idea I like is taking your teenage daughter on a date. I mean a real nice one. Dress up, drive the car around the block, pick her up, go to a nice restaurant, seat her, and initiate dinner conversation with her on things she's interested in. Such an evening will show her how much you care for her and how a young lady should be treated by a young man on a date. And because of the surprise and newness factor, it should be a lot of fun for both of you.

2. RULES/BOUNDARIES

Teenagers want rules. This statement is probably as surprising to you as it was to me. I can assure you I did not pick up this idea from my kids! "Dad, I really like your rules" and "Dad, could you please establish some tighter boundaries?" are not expressions I've heard from any of my kids.

I'm relying on the observations of people who work with teens. Dr. Ross Campbell states in *How to Really Love Your Teenager*:

> But let me tell you one crucial fact—all teenagers at some level of consciousness realize they need guidance and control from their parents. They want it. I have heard so many teenagers say that their parents do not love them because they are not strict or firm enough. And so many teenagers express their thankfulness and love to parents who showed their care and concern by their guidance and control.[8]

I also listen to what Dr. Lawrence Bauman, a clinical psychologist working extensively with teenage boys and girls, says based on his experience: "It may surprise you, but the fact of the matter is that *teen-age kids actually want rules.* I have never—repeat, never—found a kid to tell me that he didn't want any rules at all."[9]

Why do teens want rules? Because during those years filled with trial and error and embarrassment, they need family standards that establish the boundaries to operate within—a zone of operation, if you will, that provides security and protection.

The specific issues of what rules to establish and how to introduce them and enforce them are addressed in chapter 10, "Disciplining Constructively." The key point that needs to be emphasized with regard to teens is that flexibility beats rigidity in rule making and boundary setting. That doesn't mean you aren't serious about the rules or you don't enforce them. That means you take into account changing circumstances, especially as your kids get older. Don't be unbending except on the few absolutes. If you really concentrate on majoring on the majors, many of the minors will take care of themselves.

Just one suggestion on the type of rules teens may welcome. Rather than dictate generalized don'ts about behavior at parties, discuss with them some real situations they might encounter and give them a way out. For example, if drugs are introduced or sexual activity is beginning, tell them to call home and you'll pick them up. Many times kids want an out—to be able to say, "Yeah, my parents don't allow this." It won't always be true or always work. But at least give them the opportunity to have some of these "outs" available when needed.

3. INDEPENDENCE/BEING TRUSTED

Independence. That's a major theme of the teenage years. What we may see as rebellion really isn't; rather, it is part of every person's natural struggle for an independent identity. Forming a separate ego identity is the central development task for teens.

If you're like me, you have ambivalent feelings about this. Sure, you know each child has to develop an independent identity, and thus, you want to see it happen. But another part of you is saddened by the loss of intimacy that you shared with your children when they were young and you were king of their world.

Hard as it may be, we must let our minds rule over our emotions. We know what's going on in those years. Our children are answering for themselves some of life's BIG questions: Who am I? What lifestyle should I adopt? What rules will I live by? What attitude will I choose? The answers are not found by researching them or by thinking for a few hours. They're forged in the crucible of life, which means it is a struggle involving the competing forces and values they find in their family, peers, school, church, and the pop culture. They will ultimately emerge with their sense of identity, conformity, authority, and responsibility.

As parents, we must do all we can to encourage and to positively support their search for these answers and their walk along the pathway to independence.

Say yes to teens as often as possible. Again, think about majoring on the majors before you say no. It means taking change in stride. Recognize and appreciate the developing independence of your teens. It means honoring the teens' personal search for values and convictions. While adolescents are experiencing and examining the options, cut them some slack. The decisions they reach within this kind of freedom will have much more validity and staying power than beliefs assumed without question.

I like Newton's Law as a principle of parenting: for each action, there is an equal and opposite reaction. In short, if I don't respond so strongly to everything my teenager does, my teen won't counter so often or with such gusto. As adults, we have the responsibility to de-escalate rather than escalate confrontations.

On this road to independence, teens also long to be trusted. They deeply resent not being trusted.

Trustworthiness is not something you can give your teens. But you can provide opportunities to be trusted—starting as early as possible. Most kids will go overboard to earn their parents' trust.

Children also pick up on attitudes of distrust and suspicion. They'll think, *Okay, if that's the way Dad thinks I am, I might as well be that way.*

Let's take a homely example but one that is often a contentious issue: trusting them in their choice of clothes. We say, "Why are you wearing *that?*" or "You can't wear that silly thing," or "Why do you have to wear what all the other kids do?" All these queries seem reasonable enough to us. Why should they follow the silly fashion dictates of their peers? Sounds reasonable. But wait. Take a look at your clothing while at work. Why are you wearing a three-foot-long thin piece of cloth wrapped uncomfortably around your neck? Or why are you wearing a totally uninteresting gray suit?

Trust them to make the decisions whenever possible. Major only on the majors.

4. PATIENCE AND UNDERSTANDING

In a survey of teens, the most common advice offered to adults was "try to understand." A sixteen-year-old pleaded, "Try to understand everything a teenager has to go through and remember that you were teenagers once, and you had to go through many of the same problems." A seventeen-year-old counseled, "Be patient. We're often unreasonable, but we try hard."

Understanding. Patience. Oh, so needed but, oh, so hard.

But whatever is hard is also likely to be well rewarded if we are successful in accomplishing it. Here's a voice of encouragement to you:

> **How can I ever thank my parents for sticking with me after all the pain I caused them: drug busts, getting kicked out of school, running away?**
>
> **I was out of control. Thank God they did not abandon me when I had abandoned myself. I owe them something. I'm going to make them proud of me!**[10]

Let's go back to the statement where we were admonished to "remember that you were teenagers once, and you had to go through many of the same problems." It's sound advice. Let your children know that you've been there, too—that you had your heart broken by a girl or that you felt miserable when you failed a big test. At a minimum, they'll know that they are not the only ones to have ever suffered from the problem—a common feeling in teens. They'll realize, hey, my dad came out of it all right. And maybe if you're lucky, they'll sense your empathy and be heartened by your love and concern.

To have patience is to exercise emotional self-control. Emotional overreaction can hurt your relationship with teens in several ways: it leads them to respect you less; it causes them to keep their distance; and it tends to push them into the influence of others.

To have patience is to wait them out in conversation. Don't jump in too quickly. They may start out talking about trivial matters, and your tendency is to cut them off. But if you wait—have patience—what's really on their hearts and minds will often emerge. It may take five, ten, or fifteen minutes, but again the wait is well worth it.

Perhaps the hardest times are when your teens don't want to talk. Fine, respect their privacy—another major need of teens. But in these silent times, teens still desperately need and want understanding. In such circumstances, perhaps you can do something that will show them you understand and you care. Give them a surprise, or grant a previously denied request. Their response to this act of understanding and love may surprise you.

I know I was surprised when my teenage son said that one of the most important virtues I have in dealing with my kids is patience. I certainly did not have this quality in my younger adult years. Eric elaborated as follows:

> **When I scream and holler and run off to my room, determined never to come out (at least until my favorite TV show is on), my dad will come into my room and tell me that he loves me. He doesn't tell me why I am wrong and try to convince me that he is right, he just tells me how he feels about it and what he thought happened. Later, when I come out (in about half an hour) I still think that I was right but I realize that it really didn't matter and I can get over it. Instead of creating a larger rupture by aggravating the situation, my dad let time take away the short-lived bitterness I felt.**

Give them understanding. Have patience with them. Lighten up!

5. AFFIRMATION

The final thing teens need is affirmation. A teen should know that "I'm someone who counts"; "I'm a valued human being."

The more affirmation teens get at home, the less they will

need to seek it elsewhere, as evidenced in this letter from a teenager:

> As most people grow up they are rarely built up and significantly put down causing intense feelings of insecurity and low self-esteem. Whenever someone is encouraged and complimented, he develops a liking for whomever has done this. People have learned how to play on each other's emotions and they will say anything the other wants to hear in order to get the things they want. In my high school youth group I had a good friend named Keri. She had litte feeling of self-worth and when Dennis came into her life he made her feel worthwhile. She knew he was an immoral person, had a child already, and had just gotten out of jail, yet she stayed with him because he made her feel good. Keri quit attending church and when I talked to her a few months later she told me she and Dennis were very physically involved. She said, "I know it is wrong but nobody else ever shows love for me in any way and so I am doing whatever it takes to keep Dennis from leaving me." It ripped my heart to see that the world is so cold that many people have to turn to things they don't believe in to feel any personal value.[11]

And dads, we have a critical affirming role to play, particularly with teenage daughters as attested to in this letter by a high school senior:

> Have you ever heard of a father who won't talk to his daughter? My father doesn't seem to

know I'm alive. In my whole life he has never said he loves me or given me a goodnight kiss unless I asked him to.

I think the reason he ignores me is because I'm so boring. I look at my friends and think, "If I were funny like Jill or a superbrain like Sandy or even outrageous and punk like Tasha, he would put down his paper and be fascinated."

I play the recorder, and for the past three years, I've been a soloist in the fall concert at school. Mom comes to the concerts, but Dad never does. This year, I'm a senior, so it's his last chance. I'd give anything to look out into the audience and see him there. But who am I kidding? It will never happen.[12]

Here we see our dad power exercised in a harmful way. The dad didn't pay attention to her, and the daughter concluded that she was dull, unintelligent, and generally boring.

So show enthusiastic, genuine interest in your teens' activities. Approve and take pride in their accomplishments.

It's really a pretty straightforward formula: you show interest in them, and they will begin to show interest in you.

POINTS TO REMEMBER
- Don't count the score at halftime.
- "After years of quiet anxiety, parents learn to their great relief that everything is A-Okay on board the spacecraft. The 'splashdown' occurring during the early twenties can then be a wonderful time of life for both generations."
- "We need help." What more do we need to hear to make the commitment to pay the necessary price?
- "Only if the emotional tank is full can a teenager be expected

to be his best and do his best."

- The fuller the tank, the more positive the feelings, the better the behavior. Be there for the refills.
- Going to the source yielded five clear-cut needs that teens are looking to their parents to fill: (1) love, affection, and a happy home life; (2) rules/boundaries; (3) independence/being trusted; (4) patience and understanding; and (5) affirmation.
- "Never once did a day pass without him saying, 'I love you.' And my dad always made sure I knew how much he loved me."
- "Let me tell you one crucial fact—all teenagers at some level of consciousness realize they need guidance and control from their parents."
- We must do all we can to encourage and to positively support teens' search for the answers to life's big questions and their walk along the pathway to independence.
- In a survey of teens, the most common advice offered to adults was "try to understand."
- "I was out of control. Thank God they did not abandon me when I had abandoned myself."
- "He doesn't tell me why I am wrong and try to convince me that he is right, he just tells me how he feels about it and what he thought happened.... Instead of creating a larger rupture by aggravating the situation, my dad let time take away the short-lived bitterness I felt."
- The more affirmation teens get at home, the less they will need to seek it elsewhere.

CHAPTER 6

FINDING THE FAMILY/WORK
BALANCE

**Could I climb the highest place in Athens, I
would lift my voice and proclaim: "Fellow
citizens, why do you turn and scrape every
stone to gather wealth, and take so little
care of your children, to whom one day you
must relinquish it all?"
—AN ANCIENT SAGE**

IN CHAPTER 1, I talked about spelling love T-I-M-E. In this chapter, we focus on work, the great obstacle to spending adequate time—to being there—with our children.

If you want to be a great dad—if you are excited about and committed to implementing a few of the action steps highlighted in this book—you have to find a healthy family/work balance. I'll be blunt. If you're working over fifty hours a week in an ongoing manner, you might as well forget these action steps. A dad working more than fifty hours a week has two major strikes against him. First, there are precious few hours to be with the kids. Second, during the hours that are spent with the kids, Dad will usually be exhausted and tense because of other pressing duties (paying bills, making repairs on the car and home, etc.).

A few words from Teddy Roosevelt are instructive. I never viewed him as a man so committed to family, but this is the finest statement I have seen on how the family/work balance should be considered:

> There are exceptional women, there are exceptional men, who have other tasks to perform in addition to, not in substitution for, the task of motherhood and fatherhood, the task of providing for the home and of keeping it. But it is the tasks connected with the home that are the fundamental tasks of humanity. After all, we can get along for the time being with an inferior quality of success in other lines, political or business, or of any kind; because if there are failings in such matters we can make them good in the next generation, but if the mother does not do her duty, there will either be no next generation or a next generation that is worse than none at all. In other words, we cannot as a Nation get along at all if we haven't the right kind of home life. Such a life is not only the supreme duty, but also the supreme reward of duty. Every rightly constituted woman or man, if she or he is worth her or his salt, must feel that there is no such ample reward to be found anywhere in life as the reward of children, the reward of a happy family life.[1]

Do fathers in America really care about finding a healthy family/work balance? The evidence points to a resounding yes. The first major study, which appeared in 1987 and was titled *Balancing Job and Homelife*, found that virtually the same percentage of fathers as mothers reported facing "a lot of stress" in balancing their work and family lives. In another 1987 survey of twelve hundred employees at a large Minneapolis company, 60 percent of the men said family concerns were affecting their work goals and plans, noting that they were often not seeking promotions and transfers because they needed to spend more time with their families. More recently, large-scale surveys of employees at Levi Strauss and American Express show that fathers are just as distressed as mothers about the difficulties of balancing work and family. Moreover, the family/work tension among men has risen dramatically since the late 1970s. According to one survey, 72 percent of working fathers were citing this tension, up from only 12 percent in 1978.

Why has the family/work tension for men increased so greatly? One reason is the increase in the number of working mothers and, consequently, the greater demands on fathers at home. A second is a greater desire by fathers to be with their children more—to play a more active, hands-on fathering role. The third reason is that more hours are being spent on the job. The average work-week rose from just over forty hours in 1973 to nearly forty-seven hours in the late 1980s. For professionals, the number of hours on the job per week is fifty-two while small-business owners and corporate executives put in fifty-seven hours a week. With such a long-term rise in working hours, it is little wonder that a survey by Massachusetts Mutual Insurance found that Americans believe "parents having less time to spend with their families" was the single most important reason for the family's decline in our society.

So it is clear that men do care—they are quite concerned. Next question: Are they doing something about it?

Here, the evidence is more mixed. Quite a number say they would like to do something about it. In 1988, DuPont surveyed 6,600 employees, half of whom were men. It found that 33 percent of the men were interested in part-time work to accommodate children, an increase from just 18 percent in 1985. In the same survey, 48 percent of the men said they would like sick-leave policies extended to cover time off to care for a sick child, up from 27 percent in 1985. A 1989 study found 74 percent of men said they would rather have a "daddy track" job than a "fast-track" job. In the last few years, the number of male employees who have stepped up to take family leave at companies has increased noticeably.

So men are beginning to move. There is a long way to go, but the direction of the momentum is evident—men want to find a healthy family/work balance, and an increasing number are ready to take action to achieve the balance.

How can it be done? What steps are involved? The steps for each person will be unique. But the first step is a common one: getting your act together. This step is absolutely foundational if you are to make any progress on balancing family and work.

GETTING YOUR ACT TOGETHER

Want to be a great dad? The starting point is to be a good man, and that involves having your life priorities straight and acting on them.

We are dealing here with the bottom line. I firmly believe that a man can be a great dad only to the degree that he has his act together emotionally and spiritually. If you want to see the best evidence supporting this statement, take a look across the American landscape and view what is happening with fathers. Millions are absent from the home—period. Scores of others are physically present but emotionally absent.

In short, millions of American fathers are dropping out, physically, emotionally, or both. Why? Because they don't have their act together. It's not that they don't love their kids or want the best for their kids. They haven't gotten themselves squared away.

Robert Bly points out that the primary experience of the American man is feeling inadequate—in your work, because "you can't achieve what you want to"; as a man, "because you don't feel that you have any close male friends, and you don't know why"; and as a husband, "because your wife is always saying that you don't talk about your feelings enough. And you don't know what your feelings are."[2]

Bly has a significant point here, but to grasp its full implications, we need to dig deeper into what he really means by knowing our feelings. In one sense, he means that we should understand our emotional feelings: joy, anger, worry, sadness, and so on. But knowing our feelings at a deeper level means understanding what really concerns us—what we think about a lot or do a lot because we value it so highly. So it gets at what we value most highly, which is another way of saying our priorities.

Getting your act together is all about thinking through, identifying, and living your life priorities.

When this has occurred, you will have balance in your life, and that balance in turn will go a long way toward helping you be a great dad, effectively implementing many of the action steps discussed in this book. Dr. Joseph Novello hit it right on the head:

> Well-intentioned but undisciplined parents can read all of the "how to discipline" tomes on the booksellers' shelves and get all of the techniques and jargon down pat; but unless they themselves provide a solid example of a well-balanced, self-disciplined adult... they have a very slim chance of raising a selfdisciplined child in an atmosphere relatively free of hassles. After all, children and teenagers respond more to what we, as adults, do, than to what we say.[3]

So that's the goal. How does it all get fleshed out in practice?

In my life, it got fleshed out in a rather messy manner in 1981 as I was confronted with a mid-life triple whammy on the job, family, and personal self fronts. After sailing along in my career, the wind got knocked out of my sails, and I languished in a windowless office with a boring job with an employer who gave no sense of direction. On the family front, there were two major pressures: kids and romance. Too much of the first and too little of the latter. It's a long story—suffice it to say that it was a year of trying to survive as we dealt with baby twin daughters and a three-year-old son. But the worst was the third part of the triple whammy, building in force and tugging away at the very center of my being: my spiritual faith was being challenged.

With all these basics of my life so out of whack, I was forced to dig deep and really ask myself, What is of ultimate value to me? What do I really want to have as my priorities—to focus my thoughts on and expend my energies on?

Actually, it was a good time to be asking those questions. For in "losing" each of the three basics in a very real sense, I could more easily gauge the greatest sense of loss.

Number one had to be God. I sensed once again as I had years previously—that life without a faith in the living God is meaningless.

LESSON: Answers to the ultimate questions of life cannot be found in career, money, fame, family, or self.

Next came family. I had turned down the job as chief economist of California. I had lost the "TRW sweepstakes" for the prestigious corporate job. I was languishing in a boring, essentially meaningless job at EPA. I was under considerable strains and drains on the home front. But I still found my home—my relationships with Carol, Eric, Krista, and Kira—to be my refuge. A source of joy, even of renewal.

LESSON: Even when the home front and family relationships are far from perfect, the family can be the refuge from the cares of the world.

Family was established firmly as number two. And thus was the priority listing established: God, family, and job.

LESSON: Knowing life's priorities and being comfortable with them and committed to them-provides a great sense of inner peace and sense of direction.

I found great comfort in knowing once again what was truly important to me. I had only to put it into practice, to live it.

And just as I started out—BOOM! From out of the blue came a job offer too good to be true. A job that would immediately put to the test my one-two-three ordering. Could job actually stay in third place when a presidential race was at hand?

The living out of my priorities, particularly in finding the family/work balance, is the focus of the rest of the chapter. I share my experience with you in some detail in the hope that it will raise some fundamental questions and issues for you to consider and will encourage some of you to take a risk in your job for the sake of your kids. I did, and I've never regretted this big decision for a moment.

TAKING A RISK TO ACHIEVE THE BALANCE

I was exhausted as I entered 1982. The combination of events and rethinking in 1981 had drained me. I just wanted to relax, to have an easy year when I could coast along.

I didn't even care so much about being stuck in my humdrum

job at EPA. Over time, it had become better as things got more organized throughout the agency. And I had been made director of the Benefits Group; I was in charge of six fellow Ph.D. economists. Not thrilling. Not really fulfilling. But all right.

I had a new perspective on my career. What I did on the job wasn't all-important. It didn't have any ultimate or eternal significance. But what I did on the home front with my wife and kids did. It was obvious to me that my energies in 1982 should be directed toward the home front. And I had peace of mind.

Then the BOOM shattered the peace. It all began innocently enough. One of my friends at EPA with whom I had commiserated in 1981 popped his head in my office and said, "I hear a senator is looking for an economist." Before I could ask for any details, he was gone. About an eight-second pop in. Isn't it amazing how such quick, seemingly insignificant events can often have such a powerful impact on your life?

Being at peace with my job was not the same as desiring to stay there the rest of my life. So within minutes after my coworker left, I was on the phone to the senator's office.

The fact that I knew very little about the senator didn't stop me. I knew enough: he was fairly young, a different type of politician who was interested in running for president. What more did I need to know?

After two preliminary staff meetings, I had my meeting with the senator. I told him that I was very enthused about the position, that I could serve him well, and all manner of other such good things. I asked for only one thing in return: that as long as I got the work done, and done well, I be allowed to leave for home each day between five and six. I told him flat out, "I want to be home for dinner with my family each night."

Such a declaration could easily have cost me the position since standard operating procedure on "The Hill"—as the Capitol area is known in Washington—is that the staff stays around as long and often as needed (or required or demanded). And there was no shortage of starry-eyed young people—many of them single who were more than willing to do whatever it took for the privilege and honor of working for a member of Congress.

Even I was a bit surprised at the risk I was taking. Particularly in light of the alternative should I not obtain the position—the interior windowless office in the mall at EPA.

Why did I do it? Because I was newly filled with the conviction that family really did come before job. Also, Krista and Kira were very active fifteen-month-old toddlers and Eric an even more active five-year-old. That meant two things.

First, I did not want to miss out on the precious moments in our children's lives when they were constantly bursting with new discoveries. Second, on a more pragmatic level, I realized that if I weren't home in the evening, things would fall apart on the home front.

Carol was back to work full-time at the State Department. Our circuits were already overloaded, even with my relaxing and flexible job at EPA. If I began to come home at 7:30 or 8:30 at night, the circuits would break. Certainly, the personal fuses would be prone to blow.

I could not allow that to happen, so I took my deep breath and told the senator about the promise I needed from him. To my surprise, he and his administrative assistant agreed. So less than two weeks later, I was roused from watching President Reagan's State of the Union address by a telephone call informing me I had the job.

Happy days are here again! What better position could I possibly be in than serving as the senator's economic advisor, carving out the economic platform for this new generation candidate of the future a man who had a great shot at being the next president of the United States?

I had arrived!

Potomac fever was high and rising once again!

All went well with the family/work balance for fourteen months. Then a bombshell was hurled my way one pleasant April day when I walked into the office of the new legislative director. I was informed that if I wished to remain a part of "the team," I had best be with "the team" at all times. He meant that I should stay at the office till around 8:00 or 9:00 each evening, come in virtually all day each Saturday, and come in many Sundays.

Knowing that he was fairly new to the office, I calmly informed him of the promise I had received as a condition of my hiring—as long as I did the work that was needed and did it well, I could be home for dinner with my family. I then cited the work I had done, which by all indications I had received was the work that was needed and was well done.

Case closed! Or so I thought. His next response was the real bombshell: "Well, that was last year, and this year is a new ball game. We're gearing up for a presidential campaign."

Hey, wait a minute, I thought. *As far as I know, games may be different each year, but the rules stay the same. The senator was there then, he knew the agreed-upon rules, and he knew where the game was heading. Nothing had changed.*

Well, I didn't know what or who was motivating the legislative director. I calmly proceeded to bring my case before "the man" himself—certain that he would remember and not go back on his word. However, I never was granted an audience with the senator. Something crowding his busy schedule always prevented it.

Finally, I received the message, somewhat indirectly through the grapevine, that the senator was not going to back me regarding his initial promise. Whether he made a conscious decision about the matter or even whether it was ever clearly presented to him, I do not know.

THE DECISION—ONE SACRIFICE NOT WORTH TAKING

What I did know was this: the choice of my career was at hand.

Do I cave in, join the team, and share in the excitement and possible glamour of the presidential race that lay ahead—what may be a once-in-a-lifetime opportunity? OR

Do I say no thanks, I don't appreciate broken promises, and the price is far too high to pay?

The decision did not come easily. I knew it could well be a turning point in my career, and I wanted to weigh the pros and cons very carefully.

I had become quite disenchanted with the senator, particularly with his character. And I wasn't about to start working sixty- to seventy-hour weeks and just kiss my family good-bye.

But, I thought, the senator does have some sound policy positions on major issues. And he does have a shot at being president. Isn't that what I had always wanted as a policy-oriented economist? The chance to be part of a presidential race with a candidate who could take off. And there was always that vision of an office in the White House. Such opportunities don't come along too often.

As for the hours, maybe all that was needed was to join "the team" awhile. Show the flag. Then when they discover that I really do not have anything to do in the evening hours or on weekends, I can slide back into my normal hours.

LESSON: It's very easy to rationalize when a tempting prize is at hand.

The thoughts on the opposing side were too overwhelming, however. First and foremost, I was a committed family man who, almost by constitution, could not sacrifice body and soul—and in the process family—to another person, however good that person or the position might be.

And that was another basic point: the senator wasn't that good. I had seen some very serious character deficiencies, which I thought would prevent him from ever becoming president. Certainly, I didn't think he would make a good president. And even more certainly, I couldn't work for someone I did not respect.

So in the end, the choice was obvious: leave and don't look back.

LESSON: If the choice boils down to career or family, choose family.

LESSON: Do not work for someone—no matter how attractive the job—you do not respect.

I made the decision in June 1983. Fine, that was behind me. Now what? What lay ahead?

GOING SOLO TO BE WITH THE KIDS

I had been so absorbed in my decision that I hadn't bothered to think about what my next job would be. When my thoughts did turn to the future, I knew it was time to leave government. I had had a full range of experiences: a prestigious congressional committee, a dynamic executive branch agency, a presidential commission, the personal staff of a senator. And after nine years of it, I had grown weary. Not total burnout—just weary.

I wanted something new. But what? My whole career had been dedicated to public policy, and I still enjoyed policy analysis and formulation. But where could I do that outside government?

There was one obvious candidate for my next employer—myself.

While I worked for the senator, I wrote a lot about the revival of entrepreneurialism in America; about all the new jobs being created from people starting their own businesses; about millions of people working out of their homes.

The notion intrigued me. I had always had an independent spirit and had always been a risk taker.

But in my career? With my income? It was serious business. It was different from always wanting to ski a new trail. Or taking unmarked shortcuts on our travels. Or even leaving government back in 1978 to write my first book. After all, I had friends scattered around the executive branch who could always land me a job when I finished writing.

I was contemplating a complete break. How does one decide to do something like that?

One begins by going back to the basics. What was really important to me? I had decided in 1981 that family definitely came before career.

After I reminded myself of that, the decision was obvious. I should strike out on my own. Go solo. Scratch that entrepreneurial itch and in the process spend a lot of time with my kids in their growing-up years.

LESSON: Follow your heart.

LESSON: If you have a vocational dream, act on it.

Big decision number two had been made. First, leave a presidential campaign, government, and a secure paycheck behind. Second, strike out on my own.

But where? Doing what? I mean, we're talking about a guy who's been in the womb for all thirty-six years of his life. First, the womb of family. Then the womb of school for twenty-one years. Then the womb of nine-to-five, weekly paycheck jobs. All nicely structured and secure.

All of a sudden, there's no structure. It's frightening. But at the same time, if you like challenges and are a risk taker at heart, it's exhilarating. What bigger risk and challenge to take on?

CAROL'S HALF OF ACHIEVING THE BALANCE

What's fascinating to me is that not too long before I made my two big decisions, Carol had made her own major career decision.

When she became pregnant in 1980, she arranged a temporary assignment to another government office in order to work part-time, which her State Department boss wouldn't allow. After the usual three months' leave following the twins' birth in October, at first she worked two days a week, then three. And she loved it. Life was fairly manageable with the arrangement.

After the detail was over and she had taken unpaid leave for two months in the summer of 1982, she started back at the State Department full-time. She worked precisely four months before she (and we) decided that it was too much. Two full-time demanding jobs and three young kids just didn't work. Something had to give.

Carol, who had tasted part-time and loved the flavor, decided that the "give" would be by her. And it would be major. She submitted a letter stating that her family situation was such that she could no longer work full-time. If they were willing to create a part-time professional position (which then did not exist), she would gladly stay on.

Remember, the letter was to the State Department. The epitome of the old-boy network in Washington, D.C. Not a department known for its enlightened personnel policies or awareness of women's concerns. So in effect, she thought it was a letter of resignation.

Miracle of miracles, six months later she was notified that the department had created a permanent, professional, part-time position, the first one ever for a nonclerical worker.

LESSON: Don't be afraid to ask for the "impossible."

THE JOY OF JOB FREEDOM

Great news. But the timing couldn't have been worse. Carol
was beginning part-time work as I was leaving the senator and the
weekly paycheck.

The bottom line in terms of income, and hence that measure
of degree of material security, was that her income was cut by
about 40 percent. So we were trying to adjust to a smaller family
income while I was starting out on my own. Not really rational,
but that's what following your heart is all about.

My searching period did not last too long. In the first week of
August, two weeks before I was to leave the senator, I received a
phone call offering me a project director position on a part-time
consulting basis. It would begin in a couple of weeks. Also, it was
a hands-on chance to work with the environmental community
in helping to build the bridge between the economic and environmental communities that I had written about in so many books
and articles.

Coincidence? Some would say so. But when you believe in a
personal God who cares about you, you know that such a surprise
offering is far from a coincidence. Hadn't I prayed for just such an
opportunity—a consulting project that was still involved with
public policy and would provide a steady income flow?

Everything was in place. At least for the next nine months,
which is how long the contract with the project ran. Beyond that?
I hadn't the foggiest notion.

Life was certainly going to be different. I was my own boss. I
could work out of my home two days a week. I could be flexible
on which days I wanted to go into the office.

Freedom! A marvelous feeling. Not only freedom in the

physical sphere—my comings and goings—but also freedom of spirit. I knew that I could more easily follow the leadings of my heart.

THE COSTS OF JOB FREEDOM

But freedom came with its costs!

Many of my friends over the past few years have expressed their envy of my freedom. I assure them it's great, but then I lay out the costs to them and ask, "Are you willing to pay them?"

The first cost is loss of material security. There is no basic, underlying income security in the life of a soloist. Every January 1, you look out on the new year, and you have no idea what you'll be doing at the tail end of it, no idea what your income that year will be, and no idea whether there will be lengthy periods of no income. That, I maintain, is not for everyone.

And I want to be honest. Even for a risk taker, one who enjoys living on the edge, there have been many times in the past nine years when high anxiety reigned. It always manifested itself by my waking up between 4:00 and 5:00 A.M. with no chance of getting back to sleep.

Such early mornings would usually come in those frequent periods when I got within two weeks of no assured future income. A project's grant would be expiring and no new project was in hand yet. That very first project was a foreshadowing of the pattern. Like a cat with multiple lives, the project received new life on seven different occasions. The exhilaration of uncertainty—of living on the edge—has its limits.

The second cost is the matter of level of income. For those who get by the first hurdle, this one almost surely trips them up. I ask, "Are you ready to take a 30 percent cut in your income? Indefinitely?"

LESSON: Maximize joy, not income.

By this time, the sheen of my freedom in the eyes of my friends has been badly tarnished.

For me, however, the third cost was the hardest to take. I anticipated the first two and was prepared to accept them when I made my decision to go solo. But the third cost came unexpectedly. It was the alienation of many of my colleagues and "friends."

I had a fantastic network of friends and colleagues throughout Washington. Folks that I had not only worked with but had shared many lunches with and had attended conferences with over the years. A consistent feature of my former jobs was that each one put me into contact with a large number of interesting people. And in Washington it's not so much what you know as who you know that matters.

I could take the step into the great consulting unknown confident that over time these friends would come through with contracts. Take good care of an old buddy—like one big extended family.

What a shock! The reality was that the majority of my phone calls the first six months went unanswered. That hurt. Deeply.

I had not experienced that too often. After all, when you call from the Joint Economic Committee of Congress, a president's commission, or a senator's office, people tend to respond quickly. I assumed it was the way the world generally worked.

What a realization to absorb: that over half my former "friends" really didn't care for me as a person; they cared only for my position. That was the really tough cost. It took its psychic toll for about a year. I finally got over it, particularly as I realized it was providing the service of clearly indicating who were my true friends and colleagues deserving of respect. But disappointment and sheer frustration were very real.

LESSON: Consider carefully who your true friends are.
Looking back on the past, starting with the risk of telling the

senator that I wanted to be home for dinner every night and continuing through the decision to leave him and then to go solo, I can truthfully say that despite the costs, I have never regretted my decisions. I always felt that if you want to be truly free, you have to be willing to take the risks. That is why I was so thrilled when I ran across this anonymous piece highlighting the connection between taking risk and personal freedom:

Think of This Today
To laugh is to risk appearing a fool.
To weep is to risk appearing sentimental.
To reach out for another is to risk involvement.
To expose feelings is to risk exposing your true self.
To place your ideas, your dreams, before the crowd is to risk their loss.
To love is to risk not being loved in return.
To live is to risk dying.
To hope is to risk despair.
To try is to risk failure.
But risks must be taken because the greatest hazard in life is to risk nothing. The person who risks nothing does nothing, has nothing, and is nothing. He may avoid suffering and sorrow, but he simply cannot learn, feel, change, grow, love, or live. Chained by his fears, he is a slave. He is not free. Only a person who risks is free.[4]

POINTS TO REMEMBER
- "Fellow citizens, why do you turn and scrape every stone to gather wealth, and take so little care of your children, to whom one day you must relinquish it all?"
- If you want to be a great dad, you have to find a healthy family/work balance.
- The direction of the momentum is evident—men want to find

a healthy family/work balance, and an increasing number are ready to take action to achieve the balance.

- A man can be a great dad only to the degree that he has his own act together emotionally and spiritually.
- Getting your act together is all about thinking through, identifying, and living your life priorities.
- Answers to the ultimate questions of life cannot be found in career, money, fame, family, or self.
- Even when the home front and family relationships are far from perfect, the family can be the refuge from the cares of the world.
- Knowing life's priorities—and being comfortable with them and committed to them—provides a great sense of inner peace and sense of direction.
- It's very easy to rationalize when a tempting prize is at hand.
- If the choice boils down to career or family, choose family.
- Do not work for someone—no matter how attractive the job— you do not respect.
- Follow your heart.
- If you have a vocational dream, act on it.
- Don't be afraid to ask for the "impossible."
- Maximize joy, not income.
- Consider carefully who your true friends are.
- "The person who risks nothing does nothing.... Chained by his fears he is a slave. He is not free. Only a person who risks is free."

PART TWO
BUILDING CHARACTER

Part 2 deals with more action steps aimed at building character in each of our children. In the early days of America, building men and women of good character, with solid values, was a principal focus of fathers. Listen to future president John Q. Adams's thoughts as expressed in a letter to his wife in 1774:

> Above all cares of this life, let our ardent anxiety be to mould the minds and manners of our children.... Pray remember me to my dear little babes, who I long to see running to meet me and climb upon me under the smiles of their mother. The education of our children is never out of my mind. Train them to virtue. Habituate them to industry, activity, and spirit.

The industrial age stripped fathers of this focus. Child raising, including the building of character and the forming of values, became exclusively the mother's domain. Dads, it is time to resurrect the best of our traditional role. Our sons and daughters, more than ever because of the powerful force of elements in our pop culture, need critical input from us to shape good character. It is a war, and the prize is the inner spirit of each child. We need to be on the front line, conducting both a defensive and an offensive on their behalf. Being on the front line means using our moments with them wisely, making a positive impression for the purpose of character building, values formation, and spiritual development.

A theme common to all the chapters in Part 2 is that we must model what we would like our children to become. Day by day, our personhood sets the tone for our parenthood. Do you want children who can love unconditionally? Love them and their mother unconditionally. Do you want to raise hope-filled children? Be hope filled. In short, live a life and lifestyle worthy of your children's emulation.

And be committed in your efforts. The "heart" you have as a dad is infinitely more vital to your children's future character, values, and spiritual beliefs than any child-rearing tactics or mechanics.

It is an awesome responsibility. But what tremendous joy can flow from seeing each child develop into a young man or young woman of great moral integrity!

CHAPTER 7

BEGINNING WITH UNCONDITIONAL LOVE

I would really hate to think that you or I might die without having really lived and really loved.
—JOHN POWELL

RALPH DROLLINGER TELLS this story about his first day of basketball practice under legendary coach John Wooden:

> I had just arrived as a freshman at UCLA to play under John Wooden, the most successful college basketball coach in history. We were fifteen former All-Americans, later to become the season's national champions.
>
> And here we were on the first day of practice… learning how to properly put on our socks and shoes. Didn't I learn this in first grade? I thought. Lesson one was with the socks. Under his close scrutiny, Coach Wooden had us carefully roll them up, like you would your shirt-sleeves. Next we laboriously unrolled them up and over our feet

toward the calf muscle. Like Sherlock Holmes with a magnifying glass, he paced the room during the process looking for a tiny, sinful wrinkle in the rows of thirty oversized white feet. He had us run our hands several times over the cotton surface to make sure we'd executed the fundamentals correctly....

Coach Wooden's philosophy stressed the proper execution of the fundamentals, which were learned by daily repetition. His approach to a seemingly complex game was simple and basic, never departing from the fundamentals.[1]

Just as lesson one in basketball under Coach Wooden was with the socks, so lesson one in building character in our children is unconditional love. That basic fundamental must be learned by daily repetition. Another great sports figure, Roger Staubach of the Dallas Cowboys, hits it right on the head when he says, "I haven't completely figured out being a parent by any means. The one thing I do know is that the bottom line is love—they have to know you love them."[2]

The key word here is *know*. Children must not only *be* loved by their parents. They must *feel* loved by their parents. Dad, this is particularly important for you to understand and act on, for it is all too easy for you to know you love your kids without them knowing it. When several thousand high school students were asked what single question they would like their parents to answer, 50 percent said they wanted to know if their parents loved them.

One of the main principles stressed in *The One Minute Father* is, "There is a big difference between being loved and feeling loved." In *The Winning Family*, Dr. Louise Hart says, "In my workshops I ask parents how many knew while they were growing up that they were loved by their parents. Many hands usually go up. Then I ask how many felt loved; fewer hands are raised." Finally, in *How to Really Love Your Teenager*, Dr. Ross Campbell relates the story of Debbie, an adolescent who tried to kill herself because she did not feel loved:

> Debbie represents a common and tragic occurrence among early adolescent girls. Debbie seemed to be happy and content during her earlier years. During those years, she was a complacent child who made few demands on her parents, teachers, or others. So no one suspected that she did not feel genuinely loved and accepted by her parents. Even though she had parents who deeply loved her and cared for her, Debbie did not feel genuinely loved. Yes, Debbie intellectually knew of her parents' love and care for her, and never would have told you that they did not love her. But Debbie did not have the precious and crucial feeling of being completely and unconditionally loved and accepted....
>
> Is it the parents' fault? Are they to be blamed? I do not believe they should be. Mr. and Mrs. Batten have always loved Debbie but have never known how to convey their love. As with most parents, they have a vague notion of the needs of a child— protection, shelter, food, clothes, education, guidance, love, etc. They have met essentially all these needs except unconditional love.
>
> I believe parents who really desire to give their teenagers what they need can be taught to do so. Parents need to learn how to genuinely and effectually transmit their love to their teenagers.[3]

I think it's always good to see both sides of an issue. Joe

White, a camp director who has worked with thousands of kids over the years, has told a story of another teenage girl that shows how unconditional love works and just how powerful it is:

> Yesterday I had an eye-opening conversation with a girl who's a model of a well-rounded, responsible, moral teenager. She told me that her mom and dad communicated to her daily how proud they were of her and how much they respected her. Cindy told me she never wanted to disappoint such a great expression of love. "Even as I went away to college and lived on my own," she said, "I always tried to do the right thing. I couldn't stand the thought of letting my parents down. They always made me feel so loved."
>
> I can't stress enough how much kids today need to see and hear and feel that unconditional love from their parents, over and over and over again. It's the pivotal need in their lives, and when it's received it forms the apex of every child's heart. It gives them the necessary strength and courage to face every pressure, day after day, for the rest of their lives.[4]

We know it's fundamental. We know it's powerful and its absence is powerful as well. We know it works. But what exactly is unconditional love?

- It's loving your child for the unique, infinitely valuable being that he or she is, regardless of performance, attitude, behavioral pattern, or specific behavior.
- It's love that is always there, regardless of the circumstances.
- It's love with no strings attached.

To your child, it's love that he or she can count on—always.

> **At the risk of being taken for granted, you made one thing crystal clear: I could count on you.**
>
> **As I speak more and more to young people around the country, I am learning that most of them don't know anything at all about that kind of consistent love or about parents they can count on. These kids don't worry about taking their parents for granted because they have never had that chance. Instead, their parents are the focus of their lives precisely because their parents can never be counted on.[5]**
>
> —Bart Campolo, in a letter to his dad

"But wait," you may be saying, "you don't know how nasty things can get around here. You don't know what my teen says to me or what she did last weekend. I mean, there's only so much a parent can take."

Right—and wrong. You have to take only so much of nasty statements or behaviors. You can despise them.

You can and should clamp down on them. But do it in love. Let your children know that though you detest what they have done, you still love them. That's possible, and that's the basic difference between unconditional love and conditional love.

On this matter of loving the child but not the behavior, I have found no more insightful words than those by Jim Sanderson in *How to Raise Your Kids to Stand on Their Own Two Feet:*

> We have to say to ourselves: "My number one priority as a mother or as a father is not to discipline my child today. It is to express love and

approval, either through words or physical touching, or both. I will find a way to do this no matter
how I feel about my child's conduct or attitude,
because I know he needs this reassurance desperately, and I need to remind myself how much I love
him. And once we have got this clear in our heads
again, we may be able to work out the disciplinary
problems in a calmer and more loving way."[6]

All right, now what? If we are agreed that we must strive for
unconditional love that our children will feel, not just know
about, how do we do it? We say it and we show it—daily!

SAYING "I LOVE YOU"

Saying "I love you" is the one practice of the many suggested
in this book that I feel I have most successfully applied. Beginning
when Eric was very young (around two or three), I have gone into
his room every night to hear him say his prayers, kiss him, and
say, "I love you." I have done this through thick and thin, regardless of the circumstances. Sometimes we've just had a verbal bat-
tle. Sometimes when mad at me, he turned his head or hid his
head under the pillow. Sometimes I've gotten out of bed at 12:30
A.M., remembering that I forgot to do it. And yes, I've even said it
on a couple of occasions when he was extremely upset and said,
"Dad, I hate you."

I really don't care what the circumstances are. I've just known
in my heart of hearts that I want the last thing that he hears each
day to be his father saying, "I love you." I'm sure the words have
had much more impact when they follow one of the "hot times"
we've had.

When did this end? Even in his teen years, I still did it and he
still liked it. How do I know? Hoping that he won't ever read this
paragraph (at least until it gets to the printer), I'll let you know—

because he often said, "Dad, aren't you going to tuck me in?" or "When are you going to tuck me in?" Those are sweet words to hear from a teen. Sweeter still are his words, "I love you, Dad," which frequently, though not always, follow my expression of love to him. There's not too much more that a dad could want from his son.

I should confess that I have not been as conscientious about this practice with my daughters. I do it with them probably about 98 percent of the time. Perhaps the difference has something to do with the fact that Eric is "by himself" whereas the girls always have each other, and that there haven't been so many tense, emotional moments with them. In any case, the 98 percent of the time is wonderful, and I love to hear their "I love you, Daddy" as I leave their room. Sometimes if I am sick and go to bed early, I'll hear Carol encouraging the kids to go upstairs and tuck Dad in.

Jim Sanderson, in his typically no-holds-barred manner, says,

> These silent signs and symbols of caring are important, but once in a while we also need to make a flat-out verbal statement of total approval. I mean to lay it out blatantly in just so many words: You are my child, and I think you are the greatest! We really do feel that way, don't we? Would we trade them for any other kids we know? OK, then let's say it without shame. Everybody else is going to qualify his admiration, restrain it out of a sense of decorum, if nothing else. And, God knows, there are enough times when the best we can muster is faint praise.[7]

Saying "I love you" can take many different forms. A popular youth speaker and author employs one that works well with his four kids:

One of the things I like to do with my children is find them busy with homework, for example, and I'll stop what I'm doing for a moment and whisper loudly, "Pssst!" They're used to it now and they never respond to it the first time, because they know what's coming.

I keep saying, "Pssst," several times, and then they start to smile and sometimes even laugh. Then they manage to put on a straight face and they'll look over at me and say, "Yeah, Dad, whadda ya want now?"

That's when I wink at them and, while never saying the words out loud, I form "Hey! I love you!" with my lips.

It never fails. They can be in a bad mood, they may have had a really bad day at school, but every time they'll break out in a smile. And then they form the same words back to me: "I love you, too!"[8]

Just how important will it be to your kids if you begin saying, "I love you," on a regular basis? Very important. First Robert Bly: "I don't know how many men have said to me, 'My father's on his deathbed and I want him to tell me that he loves me.'"[9] Now a teenage girl:

"I don't hate my dad," she said, struggling through her tears, "I love him; I really love him. I don't want to hurt him; I just want him to stop putting me down. I want him to love me as his daughter."

As we talked, she told me of the devastation she felt when her father ignored her; then how the relationship worsened when she did some things (like drinking and drugs) to get his attention. She told of one day standing in front of him and screaming, "I'm your daughter, tell me you love me!" He pushed her aside and sat down to read the paper.[10]

SHOWING YOU LOVE THEM

Saying "I love you" should be complemented with plenty of demonstrations of your love. You can spend time with your children, communicate well with them, or go out of your way to help them. But the most important and easiest way to show them in an ongoing way, preferably daily, is to hug them.

Remember the story about the boy punker who asked Josh McDowell for a hug? That's the most powerful illustration I've come across of kids' desire for hugs. So if it's what they want, let's give it to them. How much? As much as is natural.

The recommended daily requirement for hugs has been given as: four per day for survival, eight per day for maintenance, and twelve per day for growth.

Dads, please keep in mind that preteens and teenagers need hugs, too. One study found that 64 percent of the fathers demonstrated physical affection to five-year-olds each day while only 33 percent did to nine-year-olds. We must be particularly alert about continuing to show affection to our daughters. Surveys have shown that dads often forego hugs and any form of touch when their daughters turn eleven, twelve, or thirteen and begin to mature sexually. That is precisely the wrong thing to do. They need it then more than ever. It's been well documented that a girl who becomes sexually promiscuous at a fairly young age often does so because she's searching for the love she never received from her father. So hug those adolescent and teenage daughters, and don't forget the sons, either. They won't let you know at the time that they appreciate it, but they do.

> **Affection is now and always has been openly displayed in my family. My father is one of the most masculine men I know, but he always kissed my brothers and me, and he would tell us verbally how much he loved us. A lot of the boys I grew up with had fathers who were extremely uncomfortable in expressing affection to them. I suppose they were afraid it was not a manly thing to do. I do not doubt their fathers loved them; it is just they were the kind of men who only knew how to say "I love you" by getting up and going to work every day so they could provide the things their families needed.**[11]

And don't forget your wife. I had to add that since one of Carol's favorite things in life is a good hug. In fact, a poem titled "I Need a Hug" by Bruce B. Wilmer on a wall hanging I gave her probably expresses what we men should keep in mind with respect to our wives, sons, and daughters. With this reminder hanging on the kitchen wall, our kids are learning to counterattack with hugs when Carol or I am tired and cranky. Jim Sanderson wraps up the basic message about showing love in a direct, no-nonsense way:

> Is it really necessary to remind them of this fact [that we love them] so often? Unfortunately, yes. To a teenager the supply of incoming trouble and pain seldom equals the available current supply of love and reassurance. For that matter, these elements are often out of balance for adults, too—that's one

of the reasons we get married. Obviously the act of demonstrating love daily to our children can also help to stabilize our own lives.

It seems a bit shameful even to be articulating these things: they simply ought to happen. But they don't. We often have to look at the way we live and say, "That's not good enough." It struck me one day coming back from a business trip how glad I was to see my wife and children, and how eager each of them was to see me. I could hardly put my suitcase down before we were all hugging and kissing each other. Our culture had given us permission to display this feeling after a suitable absence. But… why do we have to wait? When I come home from the office now I feel that eight or ten hours away is long enough, and I give everybody a hug whether he or she is in the mood for it or not. I'm in the mood for it, and I have the right to tell them physically how I feel.[12]

Now I want to share with you a practice that powerfully demonstrates to your children that your love is unconditional. It combines saying "I love you" and showing that you love them.

GIVING A BLESSING

The practice is giving a blessing to each child in your family. Why give a blessing? Because it works. And how do I know? Because I have seen it in my family and I have heard or read the witness of many kids about the impact it has had on their lives. Listen to just one of these children:

> **Dear Dad,**
> **Let me start out by saying that I love you very**

much. I have nothing but respect for you. As a child growing up, there is no one a son looks up to more than his dad. The love and attention you showed me meant so much. I always felt I could tell you anything.

This was shown especially in your blessings which I had every night for as long as I can remember. There is so much more involved in those blessings than just the words themselves. I want you to know that when you came into my room to bless me, I felt very special. It only established my confidence and made me feel worthwhile. It made me feel that you trusted me and gave me your blessing on everything I did. When you told me to do something—for instance, to be home by a certain time—I wanted to obey because I didn't want to break your trust.

Well, obviously, I'm not the second person to lead a perfect life. I've made more than a handful of bad decisions and choices. Yet despite that, you are always forgiving and there to listen to my problems.

I consider you both a friend and a role model. I have always had fun with you. Whether it was when you were taking me out to play baseball and golf or going to my baseball games religiously, I felt great to have you there to watch me play all those years. We would go home, talk about the game, and you would listen to me brag about what a great catch or hit I made. I also enjoyed watching football with you every Sunday as we groaned, booed, and cheered the Vikings on. After the game was always the best, because I would be so keyed up to play football that we would go outside, where I would run you ragged for an hour.

It's things like that that make me realize you're not just blowing smoke when you say, "The Lord bless you and keep you, the Lord make His face shine upon you and be gracious to you, the Lord lift up His countenance upon you and give you peace, in the name of the Father, and of the Son, and of the Holy Spirit." It shows me that you really mean what you say—that I am special to you.

Actions speak so much louder than words. I can tell by the way you bless and treat me that you love me. That constant reminder every night is very special to me. Thank you for your unconditional love. It means more to me than you'll ever know.[13]

—Carlton, age twenty-one

What exactly is a blessing? The best definition I have seen is contained in a book called *The Blessing* by Gary Smalley and John Trent:

> A family blessing begins with meaningful touching. It continues with a spoken message of high value, a message that pictures a special future for the individual being blessed, and one that is based on an active commitment to see the blessing come to pass.[14]

Each of these five elements is spelled out in considerable detail in their book (which you should look at if you decide to give a blessing to your children).

You can give the blessing in one of two basic ways. The first is a formal blessing involving the laying on of hands.

I will never forget the magnificent beauty of the moments when each of my children went before my father and knelt before Grandpa, and he blessed them:

> The Lord bless you, Eric [Krista, Kira], and keep you; the Lord make His face shine upon you, and be gracious to you; the Lord lift up His countenance upon you, and give you peace. In the name of the Father, and of the Son, and of the Holy Spirit. Amen.

A grandfather blessing his grandchildren—following a tradition that dates back thousands of years, yet has just as much meaning today. There wasn't a dry eye in the room.

That particular passage from the Book of Numbers is my favorite. You can choose your own Scriptures (Appendix B in The Blessing gives others), or you can speak your own message to the child.

The second way to give a blessing is in your daily words and actions. This point was illustrated by Smalley and Trent in their list "One Hundred Homes That Gave the Blessing to Children." It was based on people's answers to their question: "What is one special way you knew that you had received your parents' blessing?" The answers surprised me and definitely encouraged me, for they are the small, everyday acts such as those I've suggested in this book. A few of the one hundred will illustrate what kids view as their parents' blessing:

> We were often spontaneously getting hugged even apart from completing a task or chore.

We went camping as a family [this response was repeated often].

They would take each of us out individually for a special breakfast with Mom and Dad.

As a family we often read and discussed the book The Velveteen Rabbit, which talks about how valuable we are.

My father loved me by loving my mother.

My dad would ask me all the time, "What would it take for this to be a 'great year' for you?" and then try to see that it was.

My father let me go with him on some of his business trips.

My father let me share in his failures as well as his successes.

My father would put a special note on our pillows when he had to go out of town on business.[15]

What is a blessing? Ultimately it is our active commitment to our children's highest good.

And that highest good, for any father and mother who love God, is that their children might know and love the Lord their God with all their hearts. What a blessing for us dads to have the privilege of passing on this marvelous blessing to each child entrusted to us!

There's no better way to summarize this chapter on the power of unconditional love than to let Dann Huff speak about how it affected his life:

When I got to the point one time of saying, "I'm going to rebel! I'm out of here! I can't deal with my folks! They don't know what they're

talking about!" I remember thinking very specifically, "I can't rebel against them—they love me too much!" And I hated them for that! Now this may sound odd, but at that point I couldn't rebel. I wasn't an angel, but I couldn't turn my back on that kind of love. I wanted to, and that's what made me angry. If there had been any flaws in the way that they loved me or any hypocrisy on their part, any dishonesty or patronizing from them, then I think I would have found my hole and escaped through it. But I couldn't find that hole....

Let me close with one statement that says it all: My dad was the best man in his three sons' weddings—and my mother would have been matron of honor had we been daughters.[16]

POINTS TO REMEMBER

- Coach Wooden's philosophy of beginning with and stressing the fundamentals should be kept in mind as you begin building character in your children with unconditional love.
- Children must not only be loved by their parents. They must feel loved by their parents.
- "I always tried to do the right thing. I couldn't stand the thought of letting my parents down. They always made me feel so loved."
- Unconditional love is loving your children for the unique, infinitely valuable human beings that they are, regardless of their performance, attitude, behavioral pattern, or specific behavior.
- Detest the action. Clamp down on it. But love the children and let them know it.
- Say to your kids as often as possible, "I love you"—and at times let go with a flat-out statement of total approval.

- "I don't know how many men have said to me, 'My father's on his deathbed and I want him to tell me that he loves me.'"
- Show your kids that you love them unconditionally in a variety of ways but most of all by frequent hugs.
- Teenagers—perhaps especially teenagers—need hugs, too, and that includes both sons and daughters.
- "When I come home from the office now I feel that eight or ten hours away is long enough, and I give everybody a hug whether he or she is in the mood for it or not."
- "Actions speak so much louder than words. I can tell by the way you bless and treat me that you love me. That constant reminder every night is very special to me."
- "A family blessing begins with meaningful touching. It continues with a spoken message of high value, a message that pictures a special future for the individual being blessed, and one that is based on an active commitment to see the blessing come to pass."
- You can give the blessing in one of two basic ways. The first is a formal blessing involving the laying on of hands while the second is in your daily words and actions.
- What a blessing for us dads to have the privilege of passing on this marvelous blessing to each child entrusted to us!
- "When I got to the point one time of saying, 'I'm going to rebel!'… I remember thinking very specifically, 'I can't rebel against them—they love me too much!'"

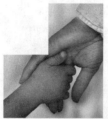

CHAPTER 8

BUILDING SELF-ESTEEM

Parents need to fill a child's bucket of self-esteem so high that the rest of the world can't poke enough holes in it to drain it dry.
—ANONYMOUS

I WANT to be honest with you—I'm nervous about writing this chapter. The topic is so significant, there's so much to say about it, and I certainly am not an expert. Scores of books have been written on this topic alone. How can one chapter suffice?

I do, however, think that I have learned a tremendous amount reading these books, and I am excited about sharing with you the common themes and lessons that emerge from them. Perhaps I can perform a worthwhile service by putting into relatively few pages the main points you should know regarding the fundamental importance of self-esteem for a child, the incredible challenges it poses for us dads, the powerful influence of culture and parents on a child's self-esteem, and the many specific actions we can take to enhance a child's self-esteem.

CHILD'S SELF-ESTEEM

em to a child? Here's what some of
:

s the single most important
ng the problems, issues, and
yday life. Self-image is cen-
d learns, achieves, works,
lf-image is the key to the
nself and is treated by oth-

...esteem is the greatest gift you can give your child—and yourself. It is the key to mental health, loving, and happiness. It is knowing that you are worthwhile and lovable.[2]

—Dr. Louise Hart

I've sifted through the complexities of countless teenagers' hearts during their times of intense crisis, and amazingly almost every tragic problem has the same root. The conversation may begin with talk about an abortion, drug addiction, or a rebellious attitude; but after a lot of time and empathy, when the layers of complex emotions are torn away, almost without fail a low self-image is uncovered.[3]

—Joe White

Self-esteem, or the lack of it, also exerts a powerful impact on the broader society:

The remarkable thing is that we really love our

neighbor as ourselves: we do unto others as we do unto ourselves. We hate others when we hate ourselves. We are tolerant toward others when we tolerate ourselves. We forgive others when we forgive ourselves. It is not love of self but hatred of self which is at the root of the troubles that afflict the world.[4]

—Eric Hoffer

Whenever the keys to self-esteem are seemingly out of reach for a large percentage of the people, as in twentieth-century America, then widespread "mental illness," neuroticism, hatred, alcoholism, drug abuse, violence, and social disorder will certainly occur. Personal worth is not something human beings are free to take or leave. We must have it, and when it is unattainable, everybody suffers.[5]

—Dr. James Dobson

Okay, that's the experts. But if you really want to understand how important self-esteem is to a child—your child—listen to Bart Campolo in a letter to his dad, Tony:

Whatever else you may have failed to do, Dad, you succeeded in making me believe without a doubt that I was the most essentially wonderful person you had ever laid your eyes on and that anyone who failed to recognize my inestimable value was simply oblivious to the obvious. You made me absolutely sure of myself. And that, more than anything else, has made all the difference in my life.

I know that some people think parenthood is all about instilling the proper principles, developing discipline, and setting a good example, but when everything is said and done, I think it has more to do with creating an indestructible sense of personal significance in a child who is going to need it for the rest of his life.[6]

TODAY'S EPIDEMIC OF INFERIORITY

We now understand how fundamentally important healthy self-esteem is to a child and to our society. The next thing to understand is that very few preteens and teens have it. Instead, amidst this group of children ages twelve to twenty, there is what Dr. James Dobson calls an epidemic of inferiority. This child development specialist, and best-selling author of numerous parenting books, notes,

> This same consuming awareness of inadequacy can be seen in every avenue of life—in every neighborhood, in each church, and on the campuses of America's schools. It is particularly true of today's adolescents. I have observed that the vast majority of those between twelve and twenty years of age are bitterly disappointed with who they are and what they represent.[7]

Why is this harsh fact true? Don't kids today have so much? True, they have "so much" in the way of things, often money, and opportunities. But they don't have the feeling of being accepted by those most significant to them. They then refuse to accept themselves, which is the root problem of poor self-esteem.

Let's get down to the real nitty-gritty of why kids aren't feeling accepted and why they refuse to accept themselves. Here's what they are up against.

First, their parents. One survey of parents revealed that dads and moms average ten negative comments to their kids for every one positive comment. Another survey, which asked parents to keep track of how often they criticize their children, found responses ranging from twenty to one hundred times a day. Now stack those facts up against the findings of experts in child psychology that it takes at least four positive remarks to offset the damage to self-esteem caused by one negative comment.

IMBED THESE RATIOS IN YOUR MIND:
P = positive comment, N = negative comment
We need to give 4P for 1N
We are giving 1P for 10N

And since we're averaging at least twenty negative comments a day, we should be giving a minimum of eighty positive comments a day to offset the damage.

And the assault on our kids doesn't end there. We're unfortunately getting plenty of negative support from the schools, another of the great consumers of our kids' time. According to one study by the National Parent-Teacher Organization, the ratio for the schools is even worse: eighteen negative comments are identified for every positive remark. Other research has found that students encounter the equivalent of sixty days each year of reprimanding, nagging, and punishment. During twelve years of schooling, a student is subject to fifteen thousand negative statements. And that is just from school professionals. It doesn't count the untold number of verbal put-downs our kids get from other kids who think such cuts are cool or humorous. It is little wonder that when kids enter the first grade, 80 percent of them feel pretty good about themselves, but by the time they get to sixth grade, only 10 percent have healthy self-esteem.

A few words on the general influence of American culture are needed to round out the picture. Although I'm convinced that parents exercise by far the most influence on children's self-esteem, strong cultural forces also are at work daily on children. Dr. James Dobson identifies physical beauty and intelligence as the two most important cultural ideals used to determine one's self-esteem and worthiness. On beauty, he points a disturbing finger at us adults: "We adults respond very differently to an unusually beautiful child than to a particularly unattractive one, and that difference has a profound impact on a developing personality."[8] No wonder that children understand the importance of physical attractiveness by age three or four. Or that when nearly two thousand girls from eleven to eighteen years old were asked, "What would you most like to change about yourself if you could... your looks, your personality, or your life?" 59 percent mentioned their looks (only 4 percent desired greater ability).

Dobson also notes that how much the ideal of intelligence affects a child's self-esteem starts with parents: "When the birth of a first-born child is imminent, his parents pray that he will be normal—that is, average. But from that moment on, average will not be good enough."[9]

The conclusion is clear: a child's self-esteem is generally not going to be enhanced by schools, peers, or America's culture. If it's going to be enhanced, it will be within the family. And here, the father has a very special role to play.

DAD'S POWERFUL INFLUENCE

In a national survey of teens dealing with how they form their self-image, the five most important variables that emerged were these:

1. A close relationship with father.
2. Spending a lot of time with father.

3. Spending a lot of time with mother.
4. Feeling secure and loved at home.
5. A grade average of A or B.

According to Josh McDowell, the survey's author, "the element that stood out is that our young people seem to place an even greater premium on their relationship with their fathers than with their mothers."[10]

I remain deeply moved and challenged by this haunting statement I read: "The perceived 'You are's of the parents become the inner 'I am's of the children."

Children are particularly affected by the father's words.

Pop singer B. J. Thomas relates the explosive negative force of words:

> **When you're six years old and your dad says for the hundredth time, "You dirty, shiftless, worthless bum, get out of here!" you believe it. You say to yourself, "Man, I'm a dirty bum, and my dad wants me to get out." That gives me a terribly negative feeling. My idol, my father, didn't like me.[11]**

And what's true for sons is even more true for daughters. Christopher Andersen, author of *Father: The Figure and the Force*, highlights the potential to destroy in a father's words:

> Clearly, the opinion any girl values most is her father's. For most little girls, Father was not only the first human being after Mother to contend

with, but the first outsider. Mother's devotion was to some extent to be expected, but Father's was more to be earned. One friend in her late 30s stands 5 feet 10 inches and weighs only 130 pounds, but she is convinced to this day that she is fat. Her father took some sort of sadistic pleasure in calling his daughter Chubby. When she tries to justify the nickname with childhood snapshots, the photos showed she was never even slightly overweight. Whatever her father's reasons for taunting her, the woman still bears the scars into middle age and appears unlikely to erase them. Similarly, a 27-year-old schoolteacher never wears short-sleeved blouses or dresses because of a disparaging comment made by her father when she was 14 about the freckles on her arms. "If it had been anyone else," she allows, "I probably would have forgotten it the next day."[12]

These statements indicate that the impact of negative words from a father does not end in childhood. Fortunately, the impact of positive words does not end in childhood, either. Eleanor Roosevelt's life story provides a perfect illustration of the finding of one study that women's achievements are directly related to the father's acceptance of them. Eleanor Roosevelt had an adoring father who was the only one building her self-esteem. "He was the center of my world," she wrote in her autobiography, "and I never doubted that I stood first in his heart." He died when she was nine, but before his death, she promised him that she would grow up to be a woman of whom he could be proud. Having fulfilled her promise many times over, she wrote at age seventy-six: "As long as he remains to me the vivid, living person that he is, he will... be alive and continue to exert his influence, which was always a gentle, kindly one."

Acceptance by father is universally sought. Don't we all, at times, wonder whether "Daddy's clapping"?

> I stand before the mirror, a fifteen-year-old girl, and belt out a song. Alone in that adolescent haven, my bedroom, I shed the self-effacing posture that is my daily accessory, throw back my shoulders, toss back my hair, and sing my heart out. "I'm the greatest star, I am by far, but no one knows it."
>
> Behind the singing teenager's reflection, there is a smiling audience of one, one who, unlike all others, appreciates my starlike qualities. Here, in the cherished privacy of my room, I entertain a fantasy, and acknowledge before the mirror my longing for his applause.
>
> Sometimes, now that I am grown and speaking of such things, I still find myself wondering, at the end of a chapter, for instance, "Daddy, are you clapping?"[13]

So dads, we have a big challenge ahead of us. Collectively, we have largely failed in encouraging in our kids healthy self-esteem. We should heed the advice that Dr. Spencer Johnson cited in *The One Minute Father*: "My two main goals as a parent are to help my children gain SELF-ESTEEM and SELF-DISCIPLINE. And in that order, the Father added."[14]

ACTION STEPS FOR BUILDING SELF-ESTEEM

Now we get to the good news, dads. There is so much we can do to build up our kids' self-esteem. Many of the ways are fun and exciting. I can virtually guarantee you that if you start putting some of them into practice, you will see a significant change in your kids, and a much happier and more peaceful household will follow.

As a lead-in to the individual steps you can take, some key statements by teens and the findings of studies are briefly highlighted. First, I'll note a sampling of teens' responses to the question: "What specific things do your parents do that make you feel good about yourself?"

> Back me up in all I do, discuss problems or joys with me, encourage me in all I do, trust me with a lot of things, spend time with me, share their life and love!

> My mom and dad will take time out of their schedules to meet my needs or to be with me. They tell me "I love you" a lot or "You're a great kid" or "I'm proud of you." They are open with me and will talk to me when I ask them to. They trust me with a lot and give me a lot of freedom to do my own things.

> What makes me feel best is that they trust me so much. They give me a lot of mature responsibility and they trust me with all their hearts. I love them so much for that trust.

> They always tell me they are proud of me no matter what I do. I've always had a problem with my grades (I'm just not a good student), but Daddy always tells me that grades are important but that communication with people is more important, and I believe that.

> They make me feel good about myself by praying with me. They encourage me a lot. They tell me that they love me.

> They congratulate me even if I fail. They try and lift my spirits.[15]

The results of the next two studies I found absolutely fascinating. Each studied the homes of children with high levels of self-esteem and came up with three main characteristics; the three were virtually identical. A study by Dr. Stanley Coopersmith of 1,738 middle-class boys and their families found these three characteristics: (1) the high-esteem children were clearly more loved and appreciated at home, with the boys knowing they were the object of pride and interest; (2) the parents had been significantly more strict in their approach to discipline; and (3) the homes were characterized by openness and democracy with freedom for individual personalities to grow and develop.[16]

The other study found that parents of highly self-confident children met three criteria: (1) they were very warm and accepting of their children; (2) they provided clear guidance; and (3) they were respectful of their children's initiatives and endeavors.[17]

Let's look now at some specific ways these can be practiced.

STEP #1: LOVE YOUR KIDS UNCONDITIONALLY.

We covered the topic of unconditional love in the previous chapter. Here we need to link it explicitly to a child's self-esteem.

Zig Ziglar, in his best-seller *Raising Positive Kids in a Negative World*, states it this way: "I have come to the conclusion that the number one cause of a poor self-image in adults and children is the absence of unconditional parental love. This unconditional love from the parents almost always precedes self-acceptance."[18] In the book *You and Your Child's Self-Esteem*, Dr. Harris says that love is one of the two basic ingredients that are "of all-consuming importance" to self-esteem.

Now, get ready for a curveball. Having just emphasized unconditional love again, following a complete chapter devoted to it, I want to stress that it may not be enough. It's what economists refer to as a necessary but not sufficient condition. The snag is that kids may know that their parents love them but not feel that they are appreciated, respected, or accepted by their parents. "After all," they reason, "they're my parents. They have to love me. But they're not really pleased with me or proud of me." Because this basic gut feeling is so prevalent, Step #2 is vital.

STEP #2: PRAISE YOUR KIDS LAVISHLY.

Get your highlighting pen or whatever else you use to mark passages, for this section is loaded with tips for turning your kids into champions, winners, optimists— all by lavishing praise and building them up.

"Nothing will do more for your child's self-esteem than a regular diet of praise"—that's the conclusion of Dr. Debora Phillips in her book *How to Give Your Child a Great Self-Image*. She cites all kinds of ways to give this praise:

- *Praise the effort.*
- *Praise the small.*
- *Praise specific acts.*
- *Praise accomplishments in the weakest areas.*
- *Praise for improving.*
- *Praise when it's least expected*
- *Praise your child just for being your child.*

Here are a couple of specific ways. Dads, compliment your children on their physical appearance, particularly your daughters (remember that 59 percent of adolescent girls chose their appearance as what they most wanted to change). Mark Twain said, "I can live for two months on a sincere compliment." Or write your children letters stating all the good you see in them and how proud you are to be their dad.

The key principle for becoming a praising father has been expressed in many catchy phrases. Dr. Spencer Johnson talks about *catching your children doing something right and giving them one-minute praisings*. The basic elements of the one-minute praisings are these: tell children specifically what they did; tell them how good you feel about what they did; pause to let them feel the good feeling; tell them you love them; and end the praising with a hug or light touch. The key insight Johnson shares through the father in his story is that his children got his attention and hugs only when they had misbehaved; "he had done nothing when the child behaved." That statement sure hit home with me. A "Dennis the Menace" cartoon perhaps expresses it best. Dennis, sitting in the corner with a tear in his eye, says, "How come I don't have a special place to sit when I do something NICE?"

Mamie McCullough talks about being *a good finder* while Zig Ziglar encourages us *to look for the gold in kids*. Ziglar got his phrase from a story he relates about Andrew Carnegie who at one point in his life was the wealthiest man in America:

> A reporter asked Carnegie how he had hired forty three millionaires. Carnegie responded that none of the men had been millionaires when they started working for him but had become millionaires as a result.
>
> The reporter's next question was, "How did you develop these men to become so valuable to you that you have paid them this much money?" Carnegie replied that men are developed the same

way gold is mined. When gold is mined, several tons of dirt must be moved to get an ounce of gold; but one doesn't go into the mine looking for dirt— one goes in looking for the gold.

That's exactly the way parents develop positive, successful kids. Don't look for the flaws, warts, and blemishes. Look for the gold, not the dirt; the good, not the bad. Look for the positive aspects of life. Like everything else, the more good qualities we look for in our children, the more good qualities we are going to find.[19]

Joe White, director of one of America's largest sports camps for kids, uses a phrase I particularly like:

After working, counselling, living, and talking with literally hundreds of thousands of teenagers in the past twenty years, I've found that there's a Champ in every one—if that child's parents will only realize it, and discover the vein of gold in their child's heart.

All successful homes have it in common: The Discovery of Champions.[20]

Champions or, as Spencer Johnson calls them, winners can not only be discovered. They can be made or at least strongly encouraged. Johnson tells how in a story illustrating his principle that the best way for children to believe they are winners is for them to see themselves winning:

"The greatest example of this," the Father said, "is the absolutely true story about the father who set things up so his small son would win—regard-less of what the child did."

The younger father laughed. "It sounds like the boy is going to grow into a real winner!"

"Of course he is!" the One Minute Father responded.

"How did the father do it?" the visitor asked.

"He taught his son how to bowl—like a lot of other fathers. However, he did things differently than most of us do with our children.

"He had the automatic pin machine set up the ten bowling pins as usual. Then, to his friends' amazement, the father set up several additional pins. He placed them at the end of the gutter."

"At the end of the gutter?" the astonished young father asked. "You did say the gutter?"

"Yes," the older man replied.

"Of course we both know that when you throw the ball so badly that it goes in the gutter, you get a zero score—because you miss all the pins."

"So why did he do it?" asked the young man.

"I'll answer your question by asking you one. Knowing that the boy was just learning and that he was only four years old, where do you think the lit-tle guy was going to throw the ball?"

The young father smiled. "I'm afraid he's going to throw it in the gutter."

"Sure. And most of us fathers would be literally 'afraid' of the same thing.

"But this father didn't care where his son's ball went. He always moved the pins in front of the ball."

The young man laughed. "I love it."

"Isn't that great? No matter where the small fry threw the ball, he was a 'winner'!"

The young man nodded his head and smiled.

"When the young man grew up, what do you think he became—other than a winner, which he did do?"

"A professional bowler"

"You guessed it. A very prosperous professional bowler! In fact, many years later, after winning more money than any other bowler on the tour, he was asked what his key to success was. Nelson Burton spoke about his father with pride.

"'I don't ever remember missing,' he said. 'I had an unusual dad!' "[21]

Why didn't I think of creative ways like that for my kids to be winners when they were younger? I'll confess: sometimes it's hard for me to rejoice when one of my children wins in a game against me.

Life, however, is not just winning. Our kids will at times lose. They will fail. How we as dads respond to these losses or failures will have a significant impact on our kids' self-esteem.

Do you get mad, upset, angry? If we're honest, we've all responded, "How could you do that?"; "You've done that perfectly before—why not now?"; "How could you do such a dumb thing?" The challenge is to minimize such responses. We should look in every such situation for ways to build up our kids.

Listen to Bart Campolo's personal story of how exciting the results can be when parents seek to build up their children. He was a young man, living on his own far from his parents, experiencing great discouragement in his first job: "I wondered how I could go on.... I felt I had completely lost my bearings and was lost at sea.... A light wind would have knocked me over." Then he says in writing to his dad, "You and Mom and Lisa [sister] showed up":

> You treated me as though I was the same successful person I had been when I left home, instead of like the complete failure I felt like just then. I remember your saying, "We are proud of you," more often than usual, and assuring me that if I couldn't make a go of it there, I could come home and work for you, Dad, because you always needed a person like me.
>
> Most important of all was Mom, who thought it all through and, right before you left, gave me a pep talk that I'll never forget.
>
> "Bart," she said, "you don't have to just stay here and feel helpless and defeated. You are a smart young man and a loving young man. But right now you have stopped looking at the people around you as people to be creatively loved, and you have started to see them only as part of a situation that is hurting you. You've become selfish. That isn't like you. You can certainly come home if you need to, but before you do, I think you need to see what God has brought you here to learn, and who He has brought you here to love and care for. Maybe you won't be a big star to everybody else, after all. But Dad and I believe in you, and we think you can make it here if you remember who you are."
>
> That visit changed everything for me. The situations did not resolve themselves overnight, of course. When you left I faced the same problems with the same deficiencies I had before (and still

have). My attitude, though, was transformed because I knew that even though I might fail sometimes, I still was infinitely valuable. Even though I couldn't solve everything, I had the ability to make a difference wherever I happened to be. Together, you reminded me of my indestructible sense of personal significance.[22]

Wouldn't it be exciting to build up our kids in that manner? To restore their self-esteem. What's tremendously encouraging from this story is that the opportunity is always there, even when our kids are grown and out the door—or even out of the city.

Catching your children doing something right. One-minute praisings. Looking for the gold. Discovering champions. Encouraging winners. Building up. Dads, start putting some of these steps into action, and change in your kids will come. Do it consistently and for a long time, and your kids will have a good sense of self-esteem and will be optimistic in their outlook on life. They will have a philosophy of life that "looks for the pony in the manure."

There is an old story told of two brothers—one a gloomy pessimist, the other a cheerful optimist. One Christmas the parents decided that they would see if they could reduce some of the differences in their two sons. So they bought for the pessimist son a roomful of the latest, most attractive toys; and for the optimistic son they stacked the barn full of manure. On Christmas morning the first son looked at the toys, complained that what he really wanted was not there, and then played with the toys for a short time before declaring he was "bored." The parents looked around for the second son and found him in the barn cheerfully and enthusiastically digging through the manure. They asked him why he was not disappointed—why he was so cheerful. His answer was, "With all this manure there's sure to be a pony here somewhere!"[23]

STEP #3: TEACH YOUR CHILDREN THAT A PERSON'S BASIC VALUE COMES FROM GOD.

For dads who believe that a person's value comes from God and that that value is infinite for all persons, this is the foundation for all self-esteem—their own and their children's. Thus, it will be of foremost importance to teach their children that they are created in the image of God, and this fact alone gives them infinite value.

STEP #4: HAVE REALISTIC EXPECTATIONS FOR YOUR CHILDREN.

My best advice here is to read the book *Children of Fast Track Parents* by Andree Brooks. I'll briefly highlight his main findings. His basic point is that it is difficult to be children of fast track parents who place high expectations on their kids. The common result is kids who become oversensitive to criticism or failure, have serious mental problems, experience chronic underachievement, suffer burnout, and have friendships characterized by competition rather than cooperation. Instead of wanting to emulate their parents' success, many feared suffering its toll. Said one boy, "My father never has any fun. Maybe he's a big lawyer. He's made a lot of money. But I don't want to be like him. I want to experience other things. When I grow old I would rather have lived a good life than become very important." Brooks concludes, "If there was one theme that constantly emerged from my conversations with the children it was a surprising undercurrent of aloneness—feelings of isolation from peers as well as parents despite their busy lives."

STEP #5: HELP YOUR CHILDREN FIND COMPENSATORY SKILLS.

All preteens and teens, to some degree, are subject to the epidemic of inferiority. One powerful way of offsetting it is for them to have a compensatory skill, something they're good at. It could be music, art, sports, student government, academics, student newspaper, whatever. It should allow them to say, "I may not be at all good in x, but I'm among the best in y."

In our family, Carol and I have thought ever since Kira was four years old that she had tremendous abilities in dance. So when she was entering fifth grade, watching her twin sister go off to a new school because she had qualified for the gifted and talented program there, we enrolled her in a top-notch ballet school. It's now one year later, and the director of the school told us that Kira should consider being a serious dancer. Most important, Kira absolutely loves ballet and jazz. Her compensatory skill blossomed at just the right time.

As a parent, you are to be constantly on the lookout for each child's hidden capacities. And when you find them, you should encourage them.

STEP #6: PREPARE YOUR CHILDREN FOR THE INFERIORITY CRISIS.

Far too often, adolescents are certain that they are the only ones who feel so "out of it," so worthless. We as dads can render a valuable service by sitting down with our kids when they're ten or eleven to tell them that a period of major change lies ahead that consists not only of physical change but strong emotional changes as well. This bit of knowledge can be of great help. And this talk can be a good time to look them straight in the eye and say, "I love you—and I'll be there with you all the way."

STEP #7: PRACTICE SPECIFIC SELF-ESTEEM BUILDING ACTIVITIES IN YOUR HOME.

I've discovered a whole host of self-esteem building practices that have proved successful for others. Here's a partial list for you to consider:

- Plant a tree in honor of a child on his birthday.
- Keep a large picture of a tree in your family room, and whenever a family member demonstrates an unusual sense of responsibility or undertakes a good deed, add a leaf, noting the event.
- Have Red Plate announcements for family members. Get a bright red plate that says, "You Are Special Today" (it can be purchased at a gift store). Then present it to acknowledge a family member's special triumphs, to praise a job well done, or to say, "You are special today."
- Spell out your admiration for a child in an acrostic. Perhaps have all family members give a positive adjective beginning with each of the letters of the chosen child's first name.
- Have a yearly formal "Family Awards" night. Everyone dresses up and a formal stage is set. Then each family member presents an award for something the assignee has excelled in over the past year. (Winners, of course, must limit their acceptance speeches.)
- Pass a candle of encouragement after dinner once a week. Light a candle at the end of a meal and pass it to a child, calling her by name and affirming something special about her. Then every other member of the family affirms her and, in turn, is affirmed.

- Start and maintain a family strength book. At the beginning of each family meeting, take a few minutes for each family member to hear compliments from the rest of the family and state a new strength for that week. Each person can maintain a notebook of personal strengths, or the father can keep a family notebook, which should be reviewed from time to time.

POINTS TO REMEMBER

- A great self-image is the single most important tool for successfully facing the problems, issues, and crises that arise in everyday life. It is central to how your child learns, achieves, works, socializes, and loves and is the key to the way your child treats himself or herself and is treated by others.
- "You [Dad] made me absolutely sure of myself. And that, more than anything else, has made all the difference in my life."
- "The vast majority of those between twelve and twenty years of age are bitterly disappointed with who they are and what they represent."
- We need to give four positive comments for every one negative comment. We are giving one positive comment for every ten negative comments.
- The cultural forces that emphasize physical beauty and intelligence are powerful destroyers of children's self-esteem.
- Two of the five most important factors cited by teens in how they form their self-image involve fathers: "a close relationship with father" and "spending a lot of time with father."
- A father's words can destroy his kids or build them up.
- The two key action steps for building self-esteem in kids are love your kids unconditionally and praise your kids lavishly.
- Catch your children doing something right, give one-minute praisings, be a good finder, look for the gold, discover champions, encourage winners, and hope that in the end they

and you will "look for the pony in the manure."

- Other action steps include these: teach your kids that a person's basic value comes from God; have realistic expectations for your children; help your children find compensatory skills; prepare your children for the inferiority crisis; and practice specific self-esteem building activities in your home.

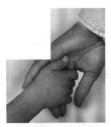

CHAPTER 9

COMMUNICATING CREATIVELY

Don't believe it when your son or daughter
tells you they "don't want to talk."
Sometimes I'll say that to my dad and mom
when they ask me how I'm doing, but I don't
mean it. I'm really hoping they will be
persistent and help me talk about it.
—GREG SMALLEY

PERHAPS a character in the movie *Cool Hand Luke* said it best,
"What we have here is a failure to communicate."
Communication—really the lack thereof—is the bane, the bone
of contention, the nadir, of so many father-child relationships.

But it doesn't have to be that way. We as dads cannot allow it
to be. Communication is too critical to leave in a state of disrepair.

I'm almost certain, particularly if you're the father of a preteen
or teen, that you're thinking, *That's fine to say. It's undoubtedly
true. But if the kids don't want to talk, there's nothing I con do. So if
that's the way they want it, let them have it.*

That's precisely the reason I began this chapter with the statement of Greg Smalley, a teenage boy, who tells us, "Don't believe it when your son or daughter tells you they 'don't want to talk.'" And he is not the exception to the rule.

Absorb the findings of a major teen survey on communication with parents:

> The Search Institute conducted an extensive study in which they asked young people this question: "If you had a serious problem in your life, who would you prefer to discuss it with to get help and gain insight'" The results indicate overwhelmingly that young people would prefer to talk to their parents in such circumstances.[1]

> Yet the reality of father-teenager communication, as opposed to what teens desire, is this:
> • Only 4 percent of teenage girls feel they could go to their fathers to talk about a serious problem.
> • When teens under stress were asked where they turn to for help in a crisis, dads were forty-eighth on the list.

The study by the Search Institute had similar bad news to reinforce these statistics. When the young people were asked who they felt they could actually approach to be listened to and taken seriously, the majority responded this way:

> **No matter how much I wish I could go to my parents, I could not. They already act toward me as if I were stupid and inadequate, and they seem to feel as if I'm always letting them down. My friends are the only ones who will listen to me and take me seriously, so I talk with them even**

though I know they don't know any more about life than I do.[2]

Now I turn to the statements of two more children to illustrate the tremendous power of either good or bad father-child communication:

> My dad rarely played games with me. He wasn't a "pal" like some fathers. He had a way, however, of getting me to talk (or listen) that worked, right up through my twenties. Every evening almost year 'round we walked a block or two to the local creamery and got ice cream cones. Those ice cream cones were an important part of my upbringing. At times we didn't say anything. Other times we argued the whole way—about whether school was better in Dad's day than in mine, or whether or not the English traditions of our family made any sense, and so on. But communication was taking place, which was the important thing. This rapport probably had a lot to do with the fact that, though I was a rebel, I never quit talking to my dad (even if I was verbally rough on him at times). Once I grew up and had a family of my own, we continued to be friends for the remainder of his life.[3]
>
> —Robert H. Baylis

> It's not that I miss my dad. I don't. I never really knew him so I can't miss him per se. What I do miss are the things we should have shared, the things we should have done together. I watch other dads and their sons. Sometimes it hurts to

watch them. I wish I could have done with my dad the things they do with theirs.

I wish I could have spent more time with my dad. I wish we could have gone bowling, fishing, or to a movie together. I wish we could have just sat and talked to each other. I never confided in my dad. We never talked about girls, dating, love, life, sex, or anything. My dad was a businessman at work and at home. He never had time for me....

I never argued with my dad. I never asked his opinion or his advice. He had zero influence on my life and life decisions, or so I thought. Now I have discovered I am just like my dad.

It's too late to change things between my dad and myself. He died eleven years ago. I wish I could tell him I'm sorry and I love him. If nothing else, he was my dad.[4]

Regretfully, Richard

MAJOR PRINCIPLES TO REMEMBER

From the child's perspective on just how critical communication is, I now turn to the many useful insights experts offer based on their extensive firsthand study of good and bad communication patterns and techniques.

Paul Tournier, the noted Swiss psychologist, expresses eloquently what lies behind the heart-cry of children for good communication with their parents:

It is impossible to overemphasize the immense need humans have to be really listened to, to be taken seriously, to be understood. No one can develop freely in this world and find life full without feeling understood by at least one person.... Listen to all the conversations of our world, between nations as well as those between couples, they are, for the most part, dialogues of the deaf.[5]

Implicit in Tournier's statement is that good communication is an essential contributor to a child's self-esteem. If you want your child to have a healthy dose of self-esteem, show her that her feelings, her ideas, her experiences, are important. If you want to see the direct relationship between self-esteem and good communication, think of the clarity of the obverse: if you don't listen attentively to a child's feelings, ideas, and experiences, you are saying in essence, "I don't value you very highly." It's as plain and as stark as that.

Good communication promotes healthy self-esteem. It also promotes character building.

"The weight of positive influence we assert on our sons and daughters will be directly proportional to the kind of communication pattern we use"—a bit of sound advice from Josh McDowell. Again, the causal relationship he is stressing is quite direct: if you want to exercise a positive influence on developing good character traits in your son and daughter, establish good communication patterns with them.

Enough said on why we should have good communication. Let's move on to how we can establish it with our sons and daughters.

In one sense, it all boils down to three major elements: listen, ask, and share. But before looking at these elements of good communication in detail, there are a few general principles to keep in mind as you become an effective communicator with your children.

PRINCIPLE #1: IF YOUR CURRENT PATTERN OF COMMUNICATION ISN'T WORKING, CHANGE IT.

Pretty basic stuff, but that's why it is being stated first. Far too many dads live with a broken communication pattern with children that has plagued them for months, if not years. Yet these same dads would not leave unattended a broken car part or home appliance.

I'm really saying here that commitment must come first. Establishing good communication patterns is going to take energy, time, and patience—commodities often in short supply. Thus, commitment must precede substance if you're going to get anywhere.

PRINCIPLE #2: LET YOUR CHILDREN KNOW THAT YOU CARE.

Children can sense very keenly when a parent doesn't really care. Whenever they do, they're going to keep quiet. If it's demonstrated to them often enough, soon they'll just tune out.

The three basic actions—listen, ask, share—show that you care. These are the positive demonstrations. Another way to show you care is to not scream at them or lecture to them. Screaming and lecturing are proven ineffective means of communication—yet they are resorted to often. As a line in a Father's Day card put it: "If I didn't have you, Dad... I'd have to lecture myself." Sarah, thirteen years old, echoes the sentiments of most teens when describing her least favorite times with Mom and Dad:

> **First, my parents scream. Then comes the we're so disappointed speech. After that, the I-never-did-that-to-my-parents-when lecture**

begins. After that, they realize how ridiculous they sounded, but they don't take back anything.[6]

PRINCIPLE #3: SEE LIFE THROUGH YOUR CHILDREN'S EYES.

Ask yourself, What does life look like to a girl whose best friend has just rejected her or to a boy who feels he's always chosen last when teams are picked? Enter your children's world. Your empathy will increase. They'll pick up on it. And before you know it, they'll be sharing with a dad who's really trying to understand them.

PRINCIPLE #4: GOOD COMMUNICATION TAKES TIME.

Sometimes it's going to take a long time. When your hurting thirteen-year-old son wants to talk about why girls aren't interested in him or your seven-year-old daughter wonders how her best friend could desert her for Jennifer, the conversation is going to take more than a few minutes. Or you may not have been hearing much of anything from one of your children—the "Silent Wonder"—for quite awhile. That may require a one-hour breakfast or lunch to get back in touch.

Fortunately, good communication can also take place in short spaces as well. Just five minutes-or maybe even one—can be plenty and plenty effective. Your one-minute openness to a child's interruption, "Listen to this, Daddy," or "What do you think about this, Dad?" can speak volumes over ten minutes of talking directed her way when you're in the mood for communicating.

PRINCIPLE #5: LOOK FOR THE GOOD TIMES FOR COMMUNICATION.

Just as important as *how* you listen or talk with your kids is *when* you listen or talk. There are good times for communication and bad times. Bad times are when you or your kids are very angry or very tired. A good time is the instant a child wants to, because most kids won't have the interest a few minutes later. Mealtimes are great for general family discussions, bedtime is particularly good for younger children, and the encouraging words you use in sending kids off to school and greeting them when they come home instill in them a positive attitude for the day.

Rhea Zahick, inventor of the Ungame, was unable to speak to her family for several months. During that time of fear and introspection, she learned five secrets of real communication: (1) listen—just listen; (2) don't criticize or judge; (3) talk from the heart; (4) don't assume that you know the other's thoughts and feelings; and (5) show your love.

Take heart from a family story where all these key points on communication come together in an exciting but very natural way:

> **In the home we weren't presented with specific dos and don'ts, but with principles that could be used to decide the specific instances we might come across. This was done casually, mainly through everyday conversations. There were many occasions for talking together. As little kids we fought to sit on Dad's knee while he and Mom drank their coffee, talking about what had happened that day. Coffee-conversation was the first order of business when Dad came home from his work as a carpenter. This tradition was continued when, as grade school children, we spent our first moments at home talking with Mom. In high school that became for some of us a coffee time sometimes lasting until supper.**
>
> **Then too, we talked around the supper table.**

Supper took a long time, but by the end of the meal we had all learned a lot about what each person was thinking. It wasn't at all an intellectual discussion (although there was room for that too), just an informal say-what's-on-your-mind time of day in which even the smallest child could participate. Noisy? Yes, but it was an important experience for us to have adults listen to us and to have adults to listen to.

Later, as we got older, we often had coffee together after the little ones had gone to bed. Here again we could test our opinions against our parents' and hear what they had to say about the world events on the ten o'clock news—and, more important, about the big events of "our world."

Nor were these the only times for talking. We talked while doing the dishes, cleaning the basement, or on the way to a picnic. When the time came that any of us really needed advice, we could bring up any subject casually, and Dad and Mom might not even notice that it was of particular concern to us.

Through talking, we gained understanding of what was important to our parents. We could learn the principles that governed their lives without ever sitting down to a lecture called "What's Important in Life." In this way, too, we learned how decisions were made, how punishments were determined. Because the principles were given in a context of usefulness, we remember them better than if they had been memorized without our being able to see how they worked out concretely.[7]

LISTEN

Out of all the thousands of sentences I've read on listening, two stand out in clearly portraying why listening is so valuable: "If you listen when they're little, they'll still be talking when the subjects are important. If you don't listen now, you may never know when the truly important things aren't being shared with you." It's a basic investment principle—if you want your return later, invest now.

Once again, the commonsense truth is not followed in practice. According to one estimate, the average parent interacting with a child talks about 90 percent of the time and the child 10 percent. You may not want to totally reverse these percentages, but it is safe to say that the largest percentage should go to the child. You need to admonish, criticize, and moralize less and listen and understand more.

As dads, we have to watch out for being too eager to jump in and "fix" the situation by providing answers or the answer.

We need to listen to the feelings of the child.

I underscore this point because it's an important one and it's a difficult one for many of us. We're all too prone to hear what's being said without really hearing what's being said. We're missing the feelings behind the words. And when this happens, we have no chance to address our children's emotions, which are often the real issue at hand.

You need to understand exactly what's being said. You don't have to accept the content, but you do have to accept the child's feelings. As Thomas Gordon, creator of the well-known Parent Effectiveness Training program puts it, let your child "own his own feelings." When your child says, "I hate you" or "I hate my sister," you remain calm and perhaps silent instead of saying harshly, "Don't ever say that again," or trying to argue, "You don't really mean that, do you?"

Just by listening, you can serve as a sounding board, helping your children process their thoughts and feelings. Listening is an effective way of extending compassion to your children.

Children are just looking for the basics: listen first, talk later. They don't care about properly phrased questions or the proper number of umm-hmms along the way to show that you are in full agreement. They want you to hear them out.

As Pat, a single mom of two teenage daughters, put it: "I have a tendency to lecture. The kids teach me that sometimes I just need to listen, to learn that I can't protect them from everything that is unpleasant and sometimes to give them the freedom to make a mistake." Bear in mind that in the very act of listening, you are learning and improving on your parenting.

There's perhaps no better way to wrap up this section on listening than to listen to the words of Eric Hoffer, the San Francisco dockworker, philosopher, and author. At age seven, he suddenly became blind, and just as suddenly, at age fifteen his eyesight returned. As he explains it, the Bavarian peasant woman who cared for him those eight years taught him the power of listening:

> This woman must have really loved me, because those eight years of blindness are in my mind as a happy time. I remember a lot of talk and laughter. I must have talked a great deal, because Martha used to say again and again, "I remember you said this.... You remember you said that...." She remembered everything I said and all my life I have had the feeling that what I think and what I say are worth remembering. She gave me that.[8]

ASK QUESTIONS

Listening is great, and it comes first. But at times you should take the initiative—become the activist by asking questions. Asking questions—at least the right kinds of questions at the right time accomplishes three things: it shows your kids you care about them, it helps you get to know them better, and properly used, it can get to the root of a problem (particularly with teens).

Always have some fun questions on hand.
- What has been your favorite book? Movie?
- What's your most prized possession?
- What's one of your big dreams?
- If you could travel anywhere, where would you go? And why?
- If a fire started in our house, what three things would you take out?
- Who are your top three heroes?
- When did you have the most fun?
- What would you do if you won $1 million?

Also keep in mind some deeper ones that will help you get to know your child better, what your child is really thinking, who he or she is down deep.
- What makes you really angry?
- What embarrasses you and why?
- When did you cry the hardest?
- If you could do three things to change the world, what would they be?
- What are five things you are really thankful for?
- What is your greatest fear?
- What three things bug you most about your friends at school?
- What brings you the greatest joy?

And when you're feeling exceptionally brave and daring, and your own self-esteem tank is pretty full, take the risk and ask:

- What do your parents do that hold you back?
- What do we do that bugs you the most?
- What do you like most about the way I'm raising you? About the way Mom is raising you?
- What do you want most from me?

When should such questions be asked? The first set of fun questions can be asked anywhere, anytime. Two particularly good spots are at the family dinner table and in the car. The whole family enjoys and learns from the answers. Perhaps your kids will want to turn the tables on you and ask you and Mom the same questions—or new ones they come up with.

The second set of questions can be asked in the same settings if you feel your children are mature enough to hear each other respectfully. If not, reserve those questions for the one-on-ones when you take a child out to breakfast or lunch or when you are driving for at least fifteen to twenty minutes in the car alone with a child. The child must be open to the questions. You're looking for communication, not an inquisition.

Questions can also be most useful in the hard times—those times our kids come to us when they have a big problem or when they're obviously hurting. I think the best advice comes from David Stone; Joe White passed along David's "Three Question" method in his book *Orphans at Home*. I am impressed when White, a man who has worked with tens of thousands of teenagers, says this about the method: "It gives amazing results, especially when used with teenagers. I've been swept off my feet to see the constructive process this method leads to in a teenager's moment of confusion. If I could encourage parents to learn and apply thoroughly only one communications technique with their kids, this would be it."[9]

Joe White suggests that you first tell your child you want to ask only three questions, but you would like to repeat them several times and each time he should give a different answer. Joe also lays out three ground rules for you: you must provide an "atmosphere of empathy," you're not to jump to conclusions and give premature advice, and you should not condemn or criticize.

Now for the three questions. The first is, What's wrong? or What do you want? The second is, What are you feeling? The key here is to discover what is going on in the heart. A "chaser" question may be necessary to clarify the feeling. For example, the interchange may be: "How are you feeling?" "I feel sad." "What's the sadness?" The third question is, What are you doing about that problem? or What are you going to do about it? After finishing with the three, start the process over again to peel off the layers and get down to the real problem.

SHARE YOURSELF

Listen. "All right, so I'll try to sit down and keep quiet for a few minutes." Ask questions. "Sure, it would be fun to learn more about what my kids are thinking." Share myself. "Hold on. That may be going a bit far. I don't even share many of my thoughts with my wife, much less my kids."

That's precisely the point. Most American men don't talk much—at least not about themselves, their thoughts and feelings. Many times I have heard my mother say, "Dad just doesn't talk with me very much." And many wives state, "My husband just won't share with me what's really on his mind." And my male friends declare, "You know, I've never shared like this with anyone before."

Somehow, we men take pride in our stoic silence—in our ability to keep it all inside—all the time depriving ourselves, our wives, and our kids of a healthy interchange of ideas and feelings. Many of us aren't in touch with our feelings. We are depriving ourselves of our full humanness.

Let's face it. If we choose to remain this way, our kids when they grow up will express thoughts along these lines:

> **Like many men, I never heard my father speak of his disappointments, longings or fears. As I came to middle adulthood I realized there was a significant dimension of my dad's life that was a mystery to him. Had I experienced emotional intimacy with Dad in my childhood and youth, it would have helped me immeasurably as a father.**[10]

You say, "Okay. Okay. I'll share myself. But what does that mean?"

It could mean talking about your job. What you actually do at work. What your frustrations are. What some successes have been. What your hopes are. What you'd really like to do in your career.

Share your thoughts on local, national, and world events and issues. Let your kids know where you stand on such issues as health care, AIDS, abortion, equal rights, homosexuality, foreign aid, cuts in school budget, proposed tax increases, candidates in political campaigns, and so on. A very attractive side benefit of such discussion is that many of the basic values you hold can be naturally shared.

After sharing has proceeded along these lines, you'll be ready for letting your kids feel your emotions. Let them know about some of your struggles, disappointments, and fears. Let them know of mistakes you've made—and the lessons you've learned from them. Of course, what you share and at what depth depend on the age and maturity of your children. Generally, I feel that kids under ten should be spared the harsher facts of life. For them, a fact like "Daddy didn't get the promotion at work he expected to and he feels really bad about it" is fine and helpful in getting them to understand that daddies have feelings, too.

For preteens and teens, at least those with a fair measure of maturity, I would encourage more in-depth sharing of struggles, mistakes, and fears. I did so throughout 1991 at some of our Sunday night family meetings, not knowing what to expect but being pleasantly surprised with all that unfolded. I let my kids know (Carol knew from private discussions) that many promising projects had not come through. That meant our financial situation was quite tight. I let them know that I was disappointed and confused about how so many promising projects could fall through one after the other. But I also let them know that "this, too, shall pass"—a basic life principle that I was pleased to convey to my kids. But rather than just saying it to them, I was striving to live it out before them.

So we—as a family—persevered. We cut back in several areas. And we prayed together that Dad would have just the right project or set of projects come his way.

And guess what? As I write this chapter, a number of interesting projects—with this book leading the way—have come together and point to a very interesting and productive period ahead.

By being open and vulnerable before my family, I taught my kids these valuable life lessons: that dads (and moms) have emotions—they can feel bad; that life is difficult at times, or as my kids would say, "It just isn't fair"; that it's okay to share these hurt feelings with others; that family members support one another; that "this, too, shall pass"; that God answers prayers, though perhaps not in our timing; and that it is good to have a firm belief in what you're doing and to persevere in pursuing your dream.

Perhaps most important, it made our family time very real and brought us much closer together as a family. I'd say that's a fine set of benefits for my willingness to be open and vulnerable.

HAVE SOME FUN

I'd like to leave you with the thought that communicating creatively with your kids doesn't have to be viewed as a heavy, burdensome, or onerous task. Have some fun with it. Look upon it as a new adventure in getting to know much better the people who are the nearest and dearest to you. Consider these fun suggestions.

Send your children notes or letters in the mail. This one was driven home to me this morning as I was reading something from my daughter in which she expressed that "I never get anything in the mail." A note of appreciation, a note of congratulations, or a note expressing how thankful you are for having the child as your son or daughter could work wonders.

If you travel, give your children a special call apart from speaking with your wife. Tell them a bit of what you're doing, what the city or the hotel is like, but most of all let them know "I miss you" and "I can't wait to see you when I get home." Your calls could make business trips less nasty in the eyes of your children.

Most of all, remember that good communication—often the best communication—can take place without a word being spoken. This fact should be encouraging news to those of you who feel a bit tongue-tied at times. The words we speak make up only 7 percent of our communications; 38 percent comes from tone of voice; and a full 55 percent is nonverbal, involving our gestures and emotions. So send out positive nonverbal messages to your kids and remember that the most powerful one will be a periodic hug or a hand on the shoulder. That sign of affection, which all children crave, speaks volumes to them.

POINTS TO REMEMBER
- Communication is too critical to leave in a state of disrepair.
- "Don't believe it when your son or daughter tells you they 'don't want to talk.'"

- "This rapport probably had a lot to do with the fact that, though I was a rebel, I never quit talking to my dad."
- "We never talked about girls, dating, love, life, sex, or anything My dad was a businessman at work and at home. He never had time for me."
- If you want your child to have a healthy dose of self-esteem, show her that her feelings, her ideas, and her experiences are important.
- If you want to exercise a positive influence on developing good character traits in your son and daughter, establish good communication patterns with them.
- If your current pattern of communication isn't working, change it.
- Let your child know that you care.
- See life through your child's eyes.
- Good communication takes time.
- Look for the good times for communication.
- "If you listen when they're little, they'll still be talking when the subjects are important. If you don't listen now, you may never know when the truly important things aren't being shared with you."
- Asking questions accomplishes three things: it shows your kids you care about them, it helps you get to know them better, and properly used, it can get to the root of a problem.
- Share yourself.

CHAPTER 10

DISCIPLINING
CONSTRUCTIVELY

When I discipline
my children, I
want them to feel
bad about their
misbehavior but
good about
themselves.
—SPENCER JOHNSON

WHEN I FIRST planned this chapter on discipline (because I knew one had to be included), I basically dreaded writing it: first, because I doubted my abilities in this important and controversial area, and second, because it seemed so negative, so distant from the joy of fathering. You see, I had fallen into the trap that ensnares so many parents—the idea that disciplining means punishing, laying down the law, making kids "shape up or ship out." I grew up with this image of discipline, and I have obviously retained it throughout most of my adult life, kind of a drill sergeant's perspective on discipline.

Now, however, I'm excited about writing the chapter. Through reading and thinking through my experience, I have gained a whole new perspective on discipline. Imagine that—at this point in my life, finally discovering the true positive definition of discipline, its basic goals, and ways it can most effectively be done. It has been an exciting and rewarding revelation for me, and if you are in the same boat as I was regarding the meaning of discipline, I hope the insights I share in this chapter will be as exciting and rewarding for you.

A NEW PERSPECTIVE

The word *discipline* is derived from the Latin word meaning "to teach" or "to instruct." Since I enjoy teaching, this concept was exciting to learn—my first obligation as a father in disciplining my children is teaching them. Teach them what? We fathers should teach our children principles and values that will help them develop an inner guidance system so they can function responsibly by themselves. In short, we discipline so they can learn self-discipline.

There's a second meaning, or aspect, of discipline. Since to discipline is "to make a disciple of," discipline also involves leadership. To discipline is to lead. To lead is to set an example. We'll see much more of what's involved in being a leader in the following section, "Preventing Misbehavior."

To discipline your children is to teach them and to lead them. Doesn't that put discipline in a much more positive light? It can be something to look forward to a positive challenge instead of a negative duty.

A third, even more unusual, meaning of to discipline is to love. Solomon, the wise king of Israel, was probably one of the first humans to link love with discipline: "He who spares his rod hates his son, but he who loves him disciplines him" (Prov. 13:24). I like the way Chuck Swindoll states the connection in *The Strong Family:* "Rather than causing your child to question your love, discipline confirms your love." He goes on to point out how numerous tests have proven that well-loved, yet well-disciplined children are healthier and have greater maturity needed to become more productive, secure adults than those raised in more discipline-free environments. Good discipline builds up children's inner strength, giving them healthy self-esteem.

Now we know the good news that to discipline is to teach, lead, and love.

But what about the kids? They certainly aren't going to view discipline so positively. And if they are going to resist it, it just won't work. Sounds logical, but fortunately, this perspective on kids is all wrong. Kids are smarter instinctively in this arena than we give them credit for. The reason: they know, in their hearts, that a parent who disciplines well—which to them means fairly and wisely—is a parent who truly cares for them and loves them. One adolescent expresses it so succinctly:

> **Why doesn't my mother ever say, "You can't go there," instead of "It's your decision"? It makes me feel frightened and alone. If she really loved me she wouldn't let me always do what I want.**

This is a cry for parents to take up their responsibilities to lead.

Here's a highly ironic fact of contemporary society: children want discipline, but many parents are afraid to give it or can't find the time for it. *Time* has pointed out how America's two most famous pediatricians, T. Berry Brazelton of Harvard and Benjamin Spock, worry about the "disappearance of discipline," particularly when both parents work. Spock observes that "parents don't want to spend what little time they have with their children reprimanding them." He also points out in his book *Dr. Spock on Parenting* how the majority of young mothers attending a conference with him soon focused their concern on how reluctant some fathers are to participate in the disciplining of their children. Spock concludes, "I had always known that there are a few fathers who evade participating in the disciplining of their children. But I was startled that a majority of the women in our group joined in the accusation and that they felt so indignant."

So dads, let's not make the same mistake that apparently many men have made. Let's enter into the job as disciplinarian with eagerness, knowing that it means being a teacher, a leader, a lover of our kids. Let's enter into it with great expectations, knowing that proper discipline brings great rewards: "Correct your son, and he will give you rest; yes, he will give delight to your soul" (Prov. 29:17).

What's great is that these rewards, promised nearly three thousand years ago, are being experienced today. Listen to E. Kent Hayes, a juvenile criminologist who has worked as a probation officer handling the no-hope cases, the superintendent of a reform school, and codirector of the National Menninger Youth Advocacy Project (a national program that places troubled children in family-care homes): "We know from hard-won experience that parents who provide the appropriate structure in their home have the happiest, most secure children. Secure children do not act out, run away, fight, or resist authority as much as those who never know the rules or what might happen next."[1]

And if all these wonderful reasons for disciplining your child do not really motivate you, just remember this. Yes, it's tough to discipline. In fact, only one thing may be tougher to do—live with an undisciplined child.

PREVENTING MISBEHAVIOR

Disciplining constructively begins with an offensive drive by the parents—an offense that tries to minimize the need for taking disciplinary action for a child's misbehavior. It's similar to a growing trend in the environment arena called pollution prevention. The beauty of pollution prevention is that since the bad stuff—pollution—is not generated in the first place, the cleanup is much simpler and less expensive for the company. To the extent that you can prevent misbehavior from occurring, the disciplinary cleanup will be much simpler and less costly in terms of frayed nerves and depleted energy levels.

We will look at four different offensive strategies: (1) modeling good behavior, (2) paying attention to and affirming children's good behavior, (3) establishing fair and well-understood rules and boundaries, and (4) tying privileges and freedom to responsibility.

1. MODELING GOOD BEHAVIOR

We begin with modeling good behavior because of the definition of discipline we learned at the outset of the chapter: discipline is an instruction to be imparted to "disciples" or learners. And how is instruction to be imparted to the disciples living with us? The method is most eloquently described by Dr. Bruno Bettelheim, the preeminent child psychologist of our time:

> For most of us, the term "disciple" is associated with Christ's Disciples, who so deeply loved and admired Him, and were so impressed by His person, His life, and His teachings that they tried to follow His example as well as they could. Their deepest wish was to emulate Him, not just because they believed in His teachings, but because of their love for Him and His love for them. Without such mutual love, the Master's teachings and example, convincing though they were in themselves, would never have been able to change the entire lives and beliefs of the Disciples.

Their story is evidence of the power of love and esteem to inspire us to incorporate another person's values and ideas in our own lives and to emulate his conduct. By the same token, the combination of teaching, example, and mutual love is most potent in preventing us from acting contrary to the value of such an individual. Following this line of thought, the most reliable method of instilling in our children desirable values and the self-discipline to uphold them should be obvious.[2]

So first, we live a life worthy of our children's emulation. To do this, we must have our own values clearly established, and we must live them. But Dr. Joseph Novello feels that where parents go wrong in disciplining children is not taking the time to establish their values as a married couple well before children arrive on the scene. Discipline, to Novello, begins with the values established by husband and wife before the birth of their first child, and maybe even before the marriage itself. Each dad should be able to stand up and say, "These are the values of our family."

The importance of having such values and living them was demonstrated persuasively in a Swedish study, which found that well-disciplined adults who live in accordance with their values hardly need to preach self-control to their children and rarely do it. It also found the converse to be true: parents who tell children to be disciplined but who lead undisciplined lives are ineffectual.

It's quite basic. If you want disciplined children, be a responsible, upright, self-disciplined person—a living example of the values you embrace.

True. And easy to say but, oh, so hard to do. I'm reminded of the poignant imagery conveyed by Robert Bly of what children get from all too many modern-day dads. He talks about how kids used to receive the father's teaching and his temperament. Now, when Dad drags himself home from the office or factory at 6:00 or possibly 8:00 P.M., the children get only his temperament. Dad's tired, and he's probably had a tough day. That's reality. It's also what great dads are called to rise above if we want to discipline our children constructively.

2. PAYING ATTENTION TO CHILDREN'S GOOD BEHAVIOR

This strategy is basic, but again it is too often neglected: pay attention to, acknowledge, and affirm children's good behavior.

All children, of any age, want attention. They so crave it that much misbehavior results from seeking parents' attention. Given these basic facts, it stands to reason that we can minimize the misbehavior by paying attention to, thereby reinforcing, the good behavior.

As dads, we give kids our attention by noticing and praising their good behavior. So they practice further good behavior to get more of our attention. Pretty soon, in a positive self-reinforcing cycle of father-child behavior, a relationship develops in which children have the confidence and the desire to do what is right.

Children will perform in the way that pays off. Encourage the good behavior by providing a big payoff for it.

3. ESTABLISHING FAIR RULES AND BOUNDARIES

The topic of establishing rules is a broad one, but two points need to be understood and applied. The first is that all families need a well-understood set of household rules—some boundaries—so that children know the territory they can operate within safely and freely The second point is what Josh McDowell calls "the number 1 rule" for parents who want to be heroes to their kids:

> Rules without Relationship Lead to Rebellion;
> Rules with a Relationship Lead to Response

How many dads have said, or are saying right now, "We have some very clear rules in our house, and my child seems to be out to break every one of them"? Why? In ninety-nine homes out of one hundred, the relationship isn't there. As Josh eloquently puts it, "Children do not respond to rules; they respond to relationships."

Let's return to point number one.

Rules are a gift to children.

Many studies have documented that children need firmly established boundaries to grow up with a healthy sense of safety and stability. This sense, in turn, allows them to experience, grow, and develop. Without rules and boundaries, there are only chaos and confusion. Thus, we are led to this paradoxical conclusion: firm and fair rules give freedom to a child.

The permissive, child-knows-best theories, which first gained popularity in the 1970s, often spawned anarchy and discord in homes. Where rules are applied and enforced in the context of a loving relationship, the child has much more freedom than the child with no constraints. I love the way Noel Stookey, better known as Paul in the famous singing trio Peter, Paul, and Mary, expresses this thought: "We understand the paradox of discipline and freedom—that you're not doing a child a service in giving him no limits. If you show him what the restrictions are, he will find ways to fly absolutely free within those limits."[3]

Remember in establishing rules and boundaries that a combination of flexibility and inflexibility is called for. Decide on the nonnegotiables. In our house, "no lying allowed" is a leading nonnegotiable. Kids want an explanation for each hard-and-fast rule, and they deserve it. With our "no lying" rule, I have explained from their earliest days that one of the most vital features of a family is to have trust with one another. As soon as lying enters the picture, that element of trust is broken, and it is a tough one to repair. Heed what Lincoln said in his final public address: "Important principles may and must be inflexible."

But as dads, we also need to be flexible—to cut some slack for our kids. Jay Kesler says yes to everything he can say yes to so that when he has something really important to say no to, he can come down with no. That makes a lot of sense to me; it is really another way of saying, "Major on the majors."

Yes, establishing rules and boundaries means learning to say a firm no—a no that is really meant and clearly understood. Again, it seems counterintuitive, but kids will appreciate it:

> I'll never forget the time, in my early teens, when I presented a wild-eyed fanciful scheme to my folks. My friend Bill French and I were going to ride our bikes across Seattle and then take the ferry across Puget Sound. Then we planned to ride thirteen miles to Panther Lake, where he and I would spend the weekend camping by ourselves. I was thirteen at the time and it all seemed like quite an adventure to me. My folks listened attentively and, when I was finished, simply said, "No." I began to walk away when Bill said to me, "Tim, you didn't even try. Come on, let's go back and explain it again. If we only badger them a little bit more, I'm sure they'll let us do it."
>
> I said to Bill, with as much security and pride as anything else, that he didn't understand. We could have stood there talking from then until doomsday and the answer would always be the same.
>
> That knowledge gave me great security as I

grew up. I can't explain it any further, except to say that I hope I pass on that same sort of strength, firmness, and security to my kids.[4]

No is a very small word, but it speaks one of life's biggest lessons: you can't (and shouldn't) always get what you want. Here are Bruce Narramore's eight guidelines for determining how to set limits on the major issues:

1. Recognize that every person is different.

2. Discuss the possible limits with your teenager before making a decision.

3. Differentiate between a biblical absolute and your personal preference.

4. Be flexible.

5. Compare your standards to those of a variety of other parents.

6. Work toward cooperative development of standards.

7. Allow increased freedom and responsibility with age.

8. Never set a limit without giving a good reason.[5]

4. TYING PRIVILEGES TO RESPONSIBILITY

A fourth way to prevent misbehavior in your children is to start early on in their lives tying privileges to responsibility. We don't live in a free-lunch world, but too many kids don't realize that. Their view of the world is that parents (and other people) are there to serve them, to meet their every desire. They believe that rewards come easy.

Do your children a favor: tie privileges and rewards to responsibilities so they can learn that personal satisfaction comes from setting small and big goals, short- and long-term goals, and then reaching them through dedicated effort. The rule that will teach them this valuable lesson is, "When you have..., then you may….," as in, "When you have picked up your room, then you may go outside to play."

Assigning chores is one of the best ways to teach responsibility and accountability to kids.

Through accomplishing genuine, helpful work, they develop such valuable qualities as perseverance and diligence, and they are rewarded with a sense of satisfaction. Placing chores in the following context will usually help children's attitudes toward them: "Mom and I work hard to provide the money needed to house, feed, clothe, and provide recreation for this family. We do this because we love you so and value our family so much. We really appreciate the contribution you can make toward the family's well-being and happiness by doing the household tasks we've given you. They really help to make things manageable. Thanks."

HANDLING MISBEHAVIOR

All is not peaches and cream in a family. The time must come when the bell tolls—when we must deal with misbehavior. We've done our best through practicing the four preventive principles above, but kids will be human. They will misbehave and break the rules. When they do, they should suffer the consequences. We must act.

So how do we handle it? How do we enforce and administer disciplinary action?

I have found from personal experience, from other dads, and from the experts that five practices should be followed in handling misbehavior: (1) care enough to confront, (2) start early, (3) condemn the behavior, not the person, (4) say it under control, and (5) be consistent.

1. CARE ENOUGH TO CONFRONT

It sounds like an oxymoron at first: caring and confronting. But disciplinary action must begin here.

In any situation where a child has misbehaved, you have five possible responses: (1) "I'll get him" is the revengeful I-win-you-lose-because-I'm-right-you're-wrong response; (2) "I'll get out" is the I'm-uncomfortable-so-I'll-withdraw stance toward conflict; (3) "I'll give in" is the I'll-yield-to-be-nice-since-I-need-your-love approach; (4) "I'll meet you halfway" is the nonjudgmental I-have-only-half-the-truth-and-I-need-your-half position of tolerance; (5) "I care enough to confront" is the I-want-relationship-and-I-also-want-honest-integrity position.[6]

Perhaps this idea is best illustrated by seeing what *not* caring enough to confront looks like. Here is the tragic admission (a combination of "I'll get him" and "I'll get out" approaches) made by Sparky Anderson, then manager of the world champion Cincinnati Reds, just before the 1975 World Series:

> "It was about two years ago. I told my boy, Lee, to get his hair cut," Anderson said. "It was long and tied in a pony tail. I'd told [him] to get his hair cut before I came home again. I came home, and it wasn't cut. He was out in the garage, on his knees, fixing his motorbike. So I told him to get it cut, and he said, 'No.'
>
> "There was no way I could win. I saw that if I wanted him to cut his hair, I was going to have to get down and whip him with my bare hands. I didn't want that. So I just walked away. I cut him off from me. I had no communication with my boy for a year. He talked to his mother, but not to me. I lost my boy."[7]

By your caring, your children know you want to maintain a

good relationship, and by your confronting, your children know that you care deeply enough to allow the natural consequences from misbehavior to flow.

2. START EARLY

If you want a decent chance at having your teenager operate basically within the boundaries, start early in disciplining your child. If a four-year-old learns he can get away with not picking up his toys or with hitting his sister, what real hope is there that the child at fourteen will follow the household rules?

When you think of this principle, just think NASA *moon mission*. An Apollo spaceflight is monitored every moment from its lift-off to the time it lands on the moon. If it goes off course at all, it is put back on track.

Minor corrections are made so big problems won't develop. The result: a 220,000-mile journey that lands right on target.

So dads, if you want your eighteen-year-olds to land right on target after a complicated life's journey, make the corrections when they're easy. Don't let them get too far off course when they're two, six, or ten. Do this consistently and you may be pleasantly surprised during their teen years.

3. CONDEMN THE BEHAVIOR, NOT THE CHILD

The objective here is to let your child know that you do not approve of, or cannot accept, her behavior but that you still love her. In fact, you may want to get radical the next time your child really blows it and begin with, "Hey, I love you," and then go on to discuss why you are disappointed and the consequences. That's a lot better than saying, "What's the matter with you?"

See the difference. The first approach lets the child know that she is not under attack—that you love her regardless of her behavior, though you don't like the behavior at all. The second approach is a frontal assault: "What's the matter with you?"

Immediately, she is made to feel helpless, powerless, and small, and that's when the defenses shoot up. She feels she must defend her worth.

The "one minute father," in the book of the same title, puts it this way: "When I discipline my children, I want them to feel bad about their misbehavior but good about themselves."

4. SAY IT UNDER CONTROL

What we're really getting at is the significance of minimizing anger and angry words. I say minimize, recognizing that no dad has the complete patience of Job. I know that I have flown off the handle, and I also know that I've always regretted it.

So the goal is to strive for composure when you see misbehavior. And you try to stay cool, even in the hottest situation. Just keep in mind five-foot Allie's demonstration of the power of this technique:

> It was a cold winter day twenty years ago when I walked into the middle of an upset in one of our houses. I can't remember all of the specifics of the incident, but I will never forget the manner in which it was handled. Allie, the family-care mother, was in the house alone. She was five feet tall, and it would be stretching it to think that she weighed more than one hundred pounds. Standing over her, yelling in her face, was Sid the barbarian. Sidney had wild blond hair and bright blue eyes, and had come to our program with a temper that was notorious. He was six four and two hundred forty-five pounds, and his massive shoulders and protruding jaw could intimidate most grown men. Allie told Sid that he could not go out that evening, because he had not done his homework or

completed his chores. He was yelling obscenities and pointing his finger. Allie stood there looking him in the eye, and talking in a calm, slow, moderate tone. He would yell he was going anyway, and she would say, "No, Sid, you need to stay home and get your homework done."

This kind of exchange continued for twenty minutes while I watched. Her quiet tone was not mocking, and the expression on her face was as calming and reassuring as the soothing voice. It was a piece of art. Sid calmed down and went to his room to study. Until it was over, neither of them knew I was there. I have since noticed that the good family-care parents seldom yell, and their instructions do not include a challenge, nor are they laced with hostility.

Sidney graduated from high school and later joined the Army. I was in the house the day he came home on his first leave. By then he was a handsome, well-groomed young man. We were all proud of him, and I saw the tears glaze his eyes when Allie walked in the kitchen. When he hugged her, her feet were two feet off the ground.[8]

I can well imagine that one of the most trying situations in which to practice this composure is when your teenage child comes rolling in at 1:15 A.M. instead of the midnight hour that was agreed to. The worry and fears have built up and up. Then you see him drive up and you're so relieved he is okay. What drove the worries? Love for him. What does he get the moment he is inside? Fury.

As I said, I haven't done it yet, but I hope I have the composure when the time comes to say, "Hey, I love you. You had me worried sick. Tell me what happened."

One easy way to say it under control is to take a time-out first.

You and your child walk away from the situation, with the clear understanding that it will be dealt with soon. The same practice holds for making decisions. It is often best to delay the decision on the punishment rather than bark, "You're grounded for a month!" A bit of time will often help you assess the rational punishment to fit the crime.

All that I'm trying to say was explained much more powerfully by Solomon: "The beginning of strife is like releasing water [through the cracks in the dam]; therefore stop contention before a quarrel starts" (Prov. 17:14). It's common sense: if the dam is about to break, you don't pour more water behind it.

A gentle response is much more persuasive than an angry one: "by long forbearance a ruler is persuaded, and a gentle tongue breaks a bone" (Prov. 25:15).

5. BE CONSISTENT

I've heard it from experts. I've heard it from "expert parents" identified in the study summarized in the book *Back to the Family*. And I've heard it from children. Besides, I've seen it work in my home. It's something with so much universality that it must have considerable validity.

Be consistent in the discipline of your children.

Stick to the rules. Follow through, even when you're tired. If you do it early on, your children soon realize that the rules really are the rules—that if they are broken, consequences will follow.

As one father in the "America's Happiest Families" survey expressed it when asked about the main ingredient in any discipline: "Consistency. If something is bad, it is always bad. If it is no big deal, then act that way."

Consistent discipline is not constant discipline. In fact, the beauty of consistent discipline is that it lessens the need for frequent discipline. If you establish fair, firm, and well-understood rules and back them with predictable consequences, you will not have the role of full-time overseer and enforcer. The whole point is to have the children discipline themselves.

One area in which this has worked in our family is TV watching. Carol and I explain the principles by which we decide if a show is good or bad, and soon our children apply them without asking. The result? Few conflicts or even discussions about TV watching. So be consistent and discipline less.

The words of Sharon, a university freshman, bring together virtually everything discussed in this chapter and thus serve as a very useful summary of how to handle misbehavior:

> **The results my parents obtained were closely tied, I think, to their consistency. I received very little physical punishment from them, and then in only the severest cases. After that I had learned, and there wasn't a second offense. Physical punishment was never to vent their wrath. It was rather to give me immediate and necessary discipline, telling me plainly that certain behavior was inappropriate. I learned in that moment that the offense was wrong, that it would always be wrong (since the discipline was never a result of my parents' frustration or anger), and that I was therefore expected not to do it again. All this was bound in our mutual love: I knew my parents**

hated to punish me and I knew I hated to dis-
please them. I personally was always immediately
reassured of their love.[9]

FORGIVENESS

Nothing in the whole realm of discipline is more powerful, or
more difficult to perform, than forgiveness. It's powerful because
it's the language of unconditional love. It's difficult because it
involves swallowing our pride and suppressing our enormous egos.

Dads, our task is to create an atmosphere of forgiveness in our
homes. If we can achieve it, our adolescent and teenage children
will feel free to come to us (and their moms) with even their most
perplexing problems because they won't have to fear guilt or
rejection.

"Wait a minute. Isn't there the slight problem that kids don't
just naturally come up to a parent and ask for forgiveness?"

True. Very true. So how do they learn to seek forgiveness?

By our example. Once again, we must lead the way by modeling this most sensitive, most fundamental aspect of human relationships. It may mean asking your wife for forgiveness in the
presence of your children. And it may mean one of the toughest
tasks of all: asking your children for forgiveness for something
you've done.

It is not easy or pleasant. But the immediate cleansing and
healing of relationship that often result—and the long-term establishment of an atmosphere of forgiveness in your home—make
the effort highly rewarding.

Do you want a model of forgiveness to encourage you? Think
about the scriptural story of the prodigal son. He took his inheri-
tance, left home, squandered all he had, and finally came back
when all else had failed. His dad saw him coming down the road,
most likely unshaven with ragged clothes and stinking from eating
with the pigs.

How did his father react? How would you react? The temptation would be to berate him: "I told you so. You just had to blow it all, didn't you? Couldn't you see what a stupid thing you were doing?"

Instead, we read,

> But when he was still a great way off, his father saw him and had compassion, and ran and fell on his neck and kissed him. And the son said to him, "Father, I have sinned against heaven and in your sight, and am no longer worthy to be called your son." But the father said to his servants, "Bring out the best robe and put it on him, and put a ring on his hand and sandals on his feet. And bring the fatted calf here and kill it, and let us eat and be merry; for this my son was dead and is alive again; he was lost and is found." And they began to be merry (Luke 15:20-24).

Such is the power of forgiveness.

POINTS TO REMEMBER
- We fathers should teach our children principles and values that will help them develop an inner guidance system so they can function responsibly by themselves.
- Since to discipline is "to make a disciple of," discipline also involves leadership.
- Kids know, in their hearts, that a parent who disciplines well—which to them means fairly and wisely—is a parent who truly cares for them and loves them.
- Yes, it's tough to discipline. In fact, only one thing may be tougher to do—live with undisciplined children.
- Disciplining constructively begins with an offensive drive by the parents—an offense that tries to minimize the need for

taking disciplinary action for a child's misbehavior.

- If you want disciplined children, be a responsible, upright, self-disciplined person—a living example of the values you embrace.
- Pay attention to, acknowledge, and affirm children's good behavior.
- Rules without Relationship Lead to Rebellion
- Rules with a Relationship Lead to Response
- Firm and fair rules give freedom to a child.
- One way to prevent misbehavior in your children is to start early on in their lives tying privileges to responsibility.
- Five practices should be followed in handling misbehavior: (1) care enough to confront, (2) start early, (3) condemn the behavior, not the person, (4) say it under control, and (5) be consistent.
- Nothing in the whole realm of discipline is more powerful, or more difficult to perform, than forgiveness. Our task is to create an atmosphere of forgiveness in our homes.
- "'Let us eat and be merry; for this my son was dead and is alive again; he was lost and is found.' And they began to be merry."

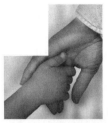

CHAPTER 11

AFFIRMING BASIC
MORAL
VALUES

**The best measure of growth for children, and
the greatest contributor to growth by other
measures, is the strength of the value system
which guides them through life.**
—JOE BATTEN

DEVELOPING PERSONAL moral values is back on the American
social agenda. Our society, families, and individuals learned that
they really couldn't do very well without them. It is a foundational truth that we lost sight of in the past twenty-five years: traditional moral values, as practiced by families and individuals for
generations, made America not only a strong country but a great
country. It is time to rebuild and strengthen our society and our
homes by the faithful teaching and practice of such timeless criteria for behavior as being honest, just, and kind.

Let us acknowledge and applaud this basic fact: moral values
work! They are powerfully effective!

The importance of basic values is instinctively understood by every parent who wants children to grow up to be moral, responsible human beings. A wonderful Yiddish word captures this goal we all share: *mensch*. In his insightful book, *Raising Your Child to Be a Mensch*, Neil Kurshan defines what being a mensch is all about:

> Menschlichkeit is responsibility fused with compassion, a sense that one's own personal needs and desires are limited by the needs and desires of other people. A mensch acts with self-restraint and humility, always sensitive to the feelings and thoughts of others. As menschen we feel a genuine passion to alleviate the pain and suffering of those around us.[1]

Look across the American landscape and you will quickly see a lack of decency, responsibility, and kindness in personal lives. Youths who have inherited or bought into the new amorality of the 1970s and 1980s—the code that basically says, "Forget traditional values and define your own rules"—have not developed a new meaningfulness. Rather, they are suffering deeply from emptiness. The results are the epidemics we've witnessed in drugs, alcohol, and teen pregnancies and the most ultimate expression of a moral nothingness, increasing teen suicide and more murders committed on a whim. Life itself, without a moral foundation, becomes cheap and disposable.

In a nutshell, most of the critical problems afflicting American youths today directly reflect a fundamental breakdown in a cohesive set of values and standards that give meaning, order, and basic dignity to life.

But enough of the problem, for the solution is at hand. A definite movement is afoot to reassert and reestablish traditional moral values in our families and in society at large. Dr. Joseph

Novello, in *Bringing Up Kids American Style*, notes,

> I sense a tremendous undercurrent of belief in many of our traditional American values such as personal freedom with accountability, the family as basic to personal happiness, self-motivation and initiative, the work ethic, the importance of religious beliefs, self-discipline, and a sense of honesty and decent morality.[2]

Jeane Westin's description of her personal transformation in *The Coming Parent Revolution* is indicative of what is happening to many middle-aged baby boomers:

> I had my own phobia about causing hang-ups when it came to moral instruction. What had happened to me in those years since my daughter was born? Age, I suppose. Then there were assassinations, Vietnam, corruption in high office—disillusionment. The old traditional morality hadn't worked, I thought, blaming the code instead of its violators—a favorite moral defense of the 1970s.
>
> But now I question the doctrine I once thought liberating, the doctrine that values are entirely personal, each person's values having the same value as anyone else's. I have reclaimed the right to make moral judgments about behavior, both public and private. Although I would defend an individual's right to behave according to standards to which I don't subscribe, I reserve the right to teach my child, "In this family, we believe that is wrong."[3]

Many of these adults are returning to church. A *Newsweek*

article highlighting the phenomenal surge in church attendance, particularly among baby boomers, states, "Above all, the return to religion is fueled by the boomers' experiences of becoming parents and the realization that children need a place where they can learn solid values and make friends with peers who share them." In short, many adults are recognizing that values will give kids a solid foundation on which to stand.

And kids want this foundation. "One of the main cries of adolescents today is for parents to provide them ethical and moral value systems to guide them," observes Dr. Ross Campbell in his best-seller *How to Really Love Your Teenager.* Teenagers, he finds, express this in many ways: one wants a "standard to live by"; another desires "a meaning to life"; others yearn for "something to show me how to live" or "something to hold on to."

So where does a child best get this "something to show me how to live"? The answer is obvious: in the home.

The editor of *What My Parents Did Right,* a collection of testimonies by adults about their parents, writes in the epilogue: "Over and over these pieces make it clear that home is a place for instilling values."

One survey found that eight in ten Americans say they acquired their core values from the family. But two-thirds of this survey group go on to say that today's children are getting their values from television, movies, musicians, and music videos.

Moral values help our children become decent, responsible, kind human beings, and they are basic to success in life generally.

Listen to the conclusion of Dr. Robert Coles of Harvard, after a twenty-year study: parents who want to give their children the best chance for success in life will teach them strong values. And the famous psychologist Erik Erickson states, "A child cannot

develop a strong as well as adaptable and working conscience…
without being guided by adults with a reasonably convincing
consensus of ethical values."[4]

If you desire to affirm basic moral values in your home, you
should know that you have plenty of company. Jeane Westin
notes that although 96 percent of parents she interviewed believe
that American society is undergoing a steep moral decline, many
of these same parents think that a renewed and strengthened family could make a big difference with children and with society.
And the overwhelming majority of the parents think that their
most important job is passing on traditions, moral codes, and
acquired knowledge—"the fingerprints of civilization"—to their
children.

And guess where a child primarily learns to make choices of
right and wrong and to become a mensch: through a father's
training and instruction.

DAD'S POWERFUL ROLE

Fathers play a powerful role—either positively or negatively—
in shaping children's basic moral values. How well are American
men doing today?

In my newspaper clipping file are two articles capturing the
transition period that American fathers are going through. One
contains a thought-provoking quote by David Blackenham, president of the Institute for American Values:

> Lots of baby-boomer fathers are self-congratula-
> tory when they compare themselves to the dads of the
> 1950s, the kind who would never dream of changing
> a diaper. But even if they were emotionally distant,
> those '50s dads weren't morally distant. They were
> home every night. Not enough of today's dads are
> around their kids enough to be a moral presence.

That probably characterizes the vast majority of fathers. But a growing number have taken an active interest and concrete role in shaping the values of their children. In an article titled "Father: Going for Higher Goals," the point is made that many fathers take values seriously. One dad says he's encouraging his children to be "kind, warm and to share with others"; another wants his children to be "kind," "helpful," and "responsible for themselves"; another talks about having "to give your kids responsibility." Rosey Grier, the huge rough-and-tumble former defensive tackle for the New York Giants and later one of the "fearsome foursome" of the Los Angeles Rams, is a turned-on father who says he hopes to instill in his child the values of honesty, concern, confidence in his faith, and an ability to love and care for others.

Let's assume that we join Rosey and these other dads in wanting to affirm basic moral values for our children. What's involved?

RECOGNIZE YOUR GOVERNING VALUES

We have to begin by recognizing and understanding our governing moral values.

> "My son just doesn't have any values at all," complained Mr. Johnson, a Washington attorney.
>
> "Well, Mr. Johnson," I asked, "just what are the values of the Johnson family?"
>
> "Ah, well, ah…" he stammered. Inadvertently, I had caught him off guard. He hadn't really thought about this question before.
>
> "What does it mean to be a 'Johnson'?" I asked.
>
> "Well, I never thought about it that way," he admitted.[5]

If you haven't thought about what it means to be a "_____" (put in your family name), now is the time.

LIVE YOUR VALUES

We can teach and preach all we want, but if we aren't living our values, our kids will see right through us. Indeed, if kids see a hypocritical split between our words and our actions, they're quite likely to ignore the well-meaning words.

Model your values. Live your values. The point can not be stressed enough. It is the fundamental determinant of the types of values your children will hold and act upon as they grow up. The two extreme impacts, negative and positive, that dads can have are illustrated in the following comments. Frank McKinney Hubbard said, "The reason parents no longer lead their children in the right direction is because the parents aren't going that way themselves." Robert Baylis speaks of his dad:

> **Another of my dad's characteristics that made an indelible impression on me was his ethical uprightness. Regardless of how unattractive his brand of Christianity seemed to me as a teenager, I couldn't avoid the fact of his goodness. I remember arguing with a neighbor kid who was trying to cut me down and challenging him to point out any immorality in my father's life. Because of his upbringing and temperament, Dad apparently didn't have too great a difficulty avoiding the usual neighborhood sins of infidelity, profanity, and drunkenness. He was good in positive ways. He was scrupulously honest. He genuinely cared for the people who lived around us and with whom he worked. He went out of his way to do things for them.[6]**

The tough challenge of living your values is not fully captured in the saying "actions speak louder than words." The challenge goes beyond good actions to the very heart of who you are. Listen to the words of an adult son in a letter to his father, a nationally known author, speaker, preacher, and professor:

> "What you are," you concluded, "is far more important than what you do." It was a good sermon, Dad. I wish you had been there to hear it.
>
> Because of all the people I know, you derive your sense of value from what you do more than anyone. How else can you explain the ridiculous schedule you maintain, which keeps you from developing normal friendships or staying healthy or even seeing your darling son as much as you should? To everyone else you preach that to have a close relationship with God is the most important thing in the world, yet you drive yourself as though God would rather have you work for Him than be with Him. You say you sometimes wonder why you don't take personal retreats more often, but you know the answer already—you are too busy. You are too busy for your support group, too busy for your family, too busy for exercise, too busy to develop friendships with non-Christians, too busy to disciple younger believers, and, by your own admission, too busy to spend a day with God. You're so caught up with doing for God that you have no time to be with Him.[7]

Don't misunderstand me. It is not an either-or situation. The priority is on who you are whether you have a heart of integrity. Then comes the requirement to do specific activities that provide a living demonstration of who you are.

Going back to Rabbi Kurshan and his goal of being a mensch, he makes the point that menschlichkeit does not develop by itself:

> Children do not magically learn morality, kindness, and decency any more than they magically learn math, English, or science. They mature into decent and responsible people by emulating adults who are examples and models for them, especially courageous parents with principles and values who stand up for what they believe.[8]

FROM START TO FINISH

When it comes to teaching and living values, the job as a dad is never done. One writer hit home with me when he spoke of my responsibility in providing my children an enormous life experience curriculum. Here are the "courses of study" in which we are tutoring our children:

1. How valuable I am.
2. What a man is.
3. What a woman is.
4. How a man and a woman relate to each other.
5. How needs are met.
6. How safe the world is.
7. How to keep responsibilities.
8. How to wait for things I really want.
9. Who you can trust.
10. How competent I am.[9]

SOME KEY MORAL VALUES

What are the basic moral values that dads should affirm in their children? Obviously, no standard list exists. Every dad, in conjunction with Mom when possible, will have his own list. I am trying to affirm three fundamental moral values for my children: (1) integrity/goodness; (2) caring for others/responsibility; and (3) learning through failures/overcoming difficulties. And I have learned from the men I have talked with and the books and articles I have read that these three values are shared by many dads.

1. INTEGRITY/GOODNESS

One of my fondest hopes for my children is that each will be a person of integrity—someone who is rooted in solid principles and will stick to them no matter what the circumstances or the crowd.

A key element of integrity is honesty. I want my children to have commitment to truth and strong consciences. I want them to have the type of commitment to truth that was instilled in Charles Colson by his dad, a commitment that was not abandoned in the severest of trials:

> "Just one thing," he would always add. "There is nothing more important than telling the truth. Always tell the truth."
>
> Those words and my dad's faithful example over the years stayed with me through adulthood and the White House-magnitude struggles I never could have imagined as a child. And so that day in the courthouse, I took a few deep breaths, sat up straight in my chair, and gave truthful answers. I did the same thing the forty-four times I was called to testify under oath during Watergate—and, as it turned out, I was the only major Watergate figure not charged with perjury.[10]

One hint to affirm this value in your children is to always

congratulate them for telling the truth, even when they are admitting misbehavior, and perhaps especially then. And when they stand by their principles, congratulate them. The building of integrity in today's world needs such affirmation.

Integrity is closely related to goodness. The goodness I am referring to is not goodness in the sense that children should "be good" and do as they are told.

> **I mean goodness of character: an adherence to fundamental moral principles, a kind nature, a pure heart.**

The opening verses of Proverbs point to the type of goodness I am seeking for my children:

The proverbs of Solomon the son of David, king of Israel:
To know wisdom and instruction,
To perceive the words of understanding,
To receive the instruction of wisdom,
Justice, judgment, and equity.

With this type of goodness, children will do something not just because they can make lots of money or because it's easy or because it's "the thing to do." They will do something because it's in their hearts.

2. CARING FOR OTHERS/RESPONSIBILITY

A second value is caring for others/responsibility. Our children—and each mature human being—should have the capacity and the inner sense of responsibility to look beyond themselves and their needs and desires to meeting the real needs of others.

That "looking beyond" should begin in the family. Help them to recognize that not only are they loved by their parents, but they are needed as well—that their contribution helps and strengthens the family. They should see that they are instrumental in making the family work.

In short, don't let "that's not my job" become a common saying in your home. Keep in mind this insightful story. Share it with your kids:

> There were four people named Everybody, Somebody, Anybody, and Nobody. An important job had to be done, and Everybody was sure that Somebody would do it. Anybody could have done it, but Nobody did it. Somebody got angry about that, because it was Everybody's job. Everybody thought Anybody could do it and that Somebody would do it. But Nobody realized that Everybody thought Somebody would do it. It ended up that Everybody blamed Somebody when Nobody did what Anybody could have done.

Don't stop at the home boundaries. Teach your children to reach out to others; help them understand there is a world of suffering beyond your neighborhood and perhaps within your neighborhood as well. This understanding can take place by giving them short articles to read on homeless people in America or on global hunger. Or encourage them to watch with you the few TV specials that highlight less fortunate people in our society and abroad.

Finally, model caring and compassion for others. Here's how one dad did it:

> **One night my dad was returning home from a business trip. At the airport he observed an older couple who apparently needed some assistance.**

He learned they were traveling from Estonia to Canada and had a layover in our city. They had only a few dollars in their pockets and had no idea where to go. So, my dad invited these bewildered strangers to our home for dinner and to spend the night. The next morning, he took them back to the airport and helped them catch their connecting flight.

You can imagine how this taught me the value of being kind. Today, I attribute my compassion to the behavior I observed in my father.[11]

This dad modeled the joy of service—a joy that carried over to his daughter. An old adage goes, "We love whom we serve." And guess what—the more your children serve others in this fashion, the more they'll love themselves as well as others. Service to others is a dynamic source of self-esteem. Help children realize that they can make a difference in the world.

3. LEARNING THROUGH FAILURES/OVERCOMING DIFFICULTIES

Another value that I want my children to have is that although failures and difficulties are inevitable, they can learn from them and overcome them. They need to learn that periodic failure is essential to personal growth.

Share this little story with your children:

A highly admired and accomplished mentor was once asked by a young apprentice, "How did you become so successful?"

"Good decisions," was all the sage, older man offered.

"But how did you learn to make so many good

decisions?" the young man pressed. "Experience," his counselor explained in a word.

"And just where did you get the right kind of experience?" the hopeful beginner pressed on. "Bad decisions," his learned guide responded.

A corollary to this value is that life is tough. Too many kids grow up thinking that everything should "go their way" or "come their way." That ain't life and the sooner they learn it, the better. But along with this harsh fact of life, be sure to teach them that life's difficulties can be overcome. Attitude. Perseverance. These are the critical ingredients.

Here's another story of overcoming to share with your kids:

A young man had a strong desire to succeed in baseball. As a child he was clumsy and awkward; yet he became one of the greatest ballplayers of all time. In his early years he was shy and easily hurt, and was not outstanding at anything. He was small for his age and considered not too bright. Other boys threw rocks at him and called him names. Because he couldn't either bat or catch the ball very well, no one wanted him on their team. But he was persistent because above all else he wanted to play baseball. With his strong will power and long hours of practice he began to improve and eventually to excel, until he became one of the greatest first basemen ever to play the game. He had many in juries and illnesses, but sick or well he never missed a game. Even late in his career, unable to straighten up because of lumbago, he still got his share of hits. Once he was knocked unconscious by a wild pitch and suffered a concussion. But he played the next day and got four hits. Near the end of his playing days his hands were X-rayed, and the doctors found that he had broken every finger on both hands, some twice, but never mentioned it to anyone. The amazing thing was that through all the pain of breaks, sprains, pulled and torn tendons, muscles, and ligaments, he played as well as ever. When he began to fail rapidly because of a degenerative disease, he worked even harder so as not to be "a handicap to his team."[12]

The man was Lou Gehrig, a real testimony to overcoming difficulties.

POINTS TO REMEMBER
- "The best measure of growth for children, and the greatest contributor to growth by other measures, is the strength of the value system which guides them through life."
- Let us acknowledge and applaud this basic fact: moral values work! They are powerfully effective!
- "I have reclaimed the right to make moral judgments about behavior, both public and private.... I reserve the right to teach my child, 'In this family, we believe that is wrong.'"
- "One of the main cries of adolescents today is for parents to provide them ethical and moral value systems to guide them."
- Parents who want to give their children the best chance for success in life will teach them strong values.
- The overwhelming majority of the parents think that their most important job is passing on traditions, moral codes, and acquired knowledge—the "fingerprints of civilization"—to their children.
- A child primarily learns to make choices of right and wrong through a father's training and instruction.

- Model your values. Live your values. It is the fundamental determinant of the types of values your children will hold and act upon as they grow up.
- "'What you are,' you concluded, 'is far more important than what you do.' It was a good sermon, Dad. I wish you had been there to hear it."
- A person who has integrity is someone who is rooted in solid principles and will stick to them no matter what the circumstances or the crowd.
- Our children should have the capacity to look beyond themselves and their needs and desires to meeting the real needs of others.
- Encourage the value in your children that although failures and difficulties are inevitable, they can learn from them and overcome them.

CHAPTER 12

INSTILLING SPIRITUAL VALUES

Great men are
they who see
that spiritual is
stronger than
material force.
—RALPH WALDO
EMERSON

THE CENTRAL ROLE OF SPIRITUAL VALUES

For the purpose of this book, Emerson's quote might be paraphrased, "Great fathers are they who see that for their children spiritual forces are stronger than material forces."

So much of day-to-day life is lived in the realm of the material. The forces of the material world—rock music, drugs, sex, alcohol, and any of a host of others—can be very strong on children of all ages but particularly on preteens and teens.

You may not agree with Emerson. You may be turned off by religion. Or maybe you haven't thought about it for a while. If so, please bear with me and read through this chapter with an open mind, for the evidence building up in recent years argues persuasively for the critical importance of instilling spiritual values in your children.

Take a good look at your children, actually looking at them if possible or seeing their images in your mind's eye. What do you see? Solely physical beings? Certainly not, for your children can think. So add mental to their characteristics. What else? Your children express emotions. So add psychological. These are the "easy three" to see, which is why some dads stop here.

But look again, and you will see children (or you will someday when they reach adolescence) who are asking, What is the meaning of life? Why am I here? The questions are universal—at all times and in all places, proof indeed that each human being also is spiritual.

Put it all together and you see what most child specialists emphasize—that each child is a combination of the physical-mental-psychological-spiritual. For us dads, that means we should be concerned with how children develop in each area.

Both physical and mental development naturally dominate because of their high visibility and the importance society places on them. But here we meet with an ironic—and in the end a discomforting—reality.

As a father, you are committed to the best possible education for your children—encouraging them through their first thirteen years of school, probably investing hundreds of hours helping them with their homework and science fair projects, and finally investing up to $100,000 for their college educations. Now that's commitment to their mental development.

That's great, but it's not enough. And it's quite likely that they will discover it's not enough. Saint Augustine, acknowledged to be one of the great thinkers of history, made this poignant observation about his father's commitment to him:

No one had anything but praise for my father who, despite his slender resources, was ready to

provide his son with all that was needed to enable him to travel so far for the purpose of study. Many of our townsmen, far richer than my father, went to no such trouble for their children's sake. Yet this same father of mine took no trouble at all to see how I was growing in your sight or whether I was chaste or not. He cared only that I should have a fertile tongue, leaving my heart to bear none of your fruits, my God, though you are the only Master, true and good, of its husbandry.[1]

So you must take stock and ask, What am I doing and what am I committed to regarding my children's spiritual development? Have I helped them in answering life's BIG questions: Who am I? What am I here for? What's the meaning of life? Sadly, I would say tragically, all too many dads have a big zero on that space in their ledger.

Whether there is a zero or perhaps a few "token investments," you can make a fresh start today. And if you make this commitment to invest in the spiritual development of your children, I can guarantee you that the potential returns are the highest yields you will find anywhere. These potential returns include helping your children

- find real meaning in life.
- develop firm values with which to identify.
- become more secure in their identity.
- gain the confidence to face a hostile world.

Fortunately, you don't have to take just Emerson's word or my word regarding the importance of the spiritual in an individual's life. This fact is being increasingly recognized by Americans from all walks of life. Magazines and books are emphasizing the power of the spiritual in an individual's life and in the life of a family unit. *The Secrets of Strong Families,* written by leading family researchers Nick Stinnett and John De Frain, identifies spiritual wellness as one of the six key strengths of strong families. The authors define spiritual wellness as follows: "Whether they go to formal religious services or not, strong family members have a sense of a greater good or power in life, and that belief gives them strength and purpose."

In a study done on one hundred of America's happiest families, the findings were strikingly similar. The findings, as reported in *Back to the Family,* are unequivocal:

> Strong family life has many components. Successful families are not in complete agreement on the relative importance, or ranking, of these components. Foolproof formulas for family success don't exist. Rather, certain themes are prevalent among healthy families, for example, reliance on common sense, teaching through example, give-and-take communication, and the will to discipline, to mention a few. One theme to emerge most prominently is spirituality, or the belief in a Creator and in living by His guidelines. Nearly ninety percent of the families pointed to spirituality as a significant, if not dominant, guiding force in their lives. Although the words varied—faith, religious beliefs, Christian principles, moral foundation, church family—the idea was the same. Spirituality is the umbrella which encompasses and fosters a more loving, close-knit family.[2]

There was a great diversity of religious traditions among these families: Catholic, Presbyterian, Jewish, Pentecostal, United

Methodist, Congregational, Episcopal, Latter-day Saints, and fundamental evangelical. Amidst this diversity, the parents and children emphasized with almost one voice that the spirit of one's beliefs—rather than the specifics—is most integral to a family's well-being.

Yes, even Dr. Spock places a priority on the spiritual. He singles out television and the sciences for stripping away much of the spiritual fabric that used to shape American society and American families. He notes that in most parts of the world, materialism is balanced by spiritual values, but in America, children get their values, particularly consumerism and competitiveness, from television. The sciences appear to have taken over "much of the authority that was formerly God's" in contrast to the past when "so much in the universe was considered mysterious and known only to God" and "a far greater number of us had a strong sense of having been created in his image and of being guided every hour of the day by his concern."[3] The result? According to Spock, "we have lost much of our sense of dignity as individuals. We don't have souls anymore." Thus, he encourages parents to make "a profound difference" by teaching spiritual values throughout childhood.

So that is what some of the experts have found and what they believe. What about kids today? Do they really see the importance of religious or spiritual values? Do they believe that the spiritual is more powerful than the material?

Apparently, they do. One comprehensive survey, "The Religion of Youth," reached a conclusion regarding teenagers' concerns that would surprise most adults: we tend to underestimate their concerns about faith, values, and life goals.

Voices of youth, as usual, speak louder than surveys:

I don't think religion has made us a success as a family, but as individual human beings. Being

successful humans makes you a successful family.
—Katy, age fifteen

Our strong religious background is the center of our family, because if... you trust in God, then everything else will fall into place. Our parents really believe that God is the one that is going to see us through and that we should seek throughout our lives to trust God and to find out what God really wants us to do.
—Kimberly, age eighteen; and Chip, age sixteen

If you look at the Ten Commandments, those are the values my parents stress. If we always keep in mind these values, life will be easier.
—David, age thirteen

My parents have stressed a strong religious background. We always have our morning devotional, and we enjoy our church activities, but most importantly, we have been taught to place all of our worries in the hands of the Lord and to remember that everything has a purpose—"Thy will be done."
—Jacob, age sixteen[4]

Those are fine, articulate statements, but sometimes the greatest insight and wisdom come from the words of the very young. According to ten-year-old Tyler, "the Lord, I think, is who holds this family together." The authors of the study found those ten words best described what most of the families in the survey believe. Yet despite this near universal acknowledgment of the importance of spiritual values, many parents feel that somehow it is "not right" to "impose" or even "impart" spiritual values to their children. "Let them discover what they will on their own" is the guiding philosophy. The basic problem with such an approach is that it leads to a large number of spiritual paupers among young people. And since nature abhors a vacuum, something is going to fill the minds of children, be it the philosophy and "principles" of rock musicians or the dictates of a cult figure or the narcissistic view that life should simply be the pursuit of pleasure.

This problem is true of every generation today, not just youths. *Newsweek* has noted that the men's movement, which looks inward, "seeks to resolve the spiritual crisis of the American man."

Wouldn't it be wonderful if fathers in America would commit to heading off that type of crisis for their children by at least rooting them in time-tested, traditional spiritual values? How do you do this? I suggest a focus on just two areas: introducing your children to God and to prayer.

INTRODUCING YOUR CHILDREN TO GOD

As a dad, you can give your children many things but a relationship with God is not one of them. That ultimately has to be of their own choosing. But you can and should introduce them to God. Precisely how you do this—and with what fervor—depends on your relationship with God.

Thus, I have divided this section into two parts: the first for dads who have a solid and fervent belief in God that they would like to pass along to their children, and the second for dads who aren't sure about the existence of God or their relationship with Him but would like their children to be introduced to God so they can then render their own judgment. No matter which group you find yourself in, please read through both parts since each has points you may find applicable.

For a dad who has a strong belief in God, your first and foremost responsibility is to teach your children about God and to live a life consonant with your religious convictions. To do less is to betray all you believe and all you are.

The foundational biblical passage for fathers is Deuteronomy 6:4-9 (NIV):

> Hear, O Israel: The Lord our God, the Lord is one. Love the Lord your God with all your heart and with all your soul and with all your strength. These commandments that I give you today are to be upon your hearts. Impress them on your children. Talk about them when you sit at home and when you walk along the road, when you lie down and when you get up. Tie them as symbols on your hands and bind them on your foreheads. Write them on the doorframes of your houses and on your gates.

The system is to teach and talk. Let's look first at the teaching role. The root term for "teach" suggests repeating, telling over and over again as well as modeling a consistent message. Further, we are to teach "diligently"; the root term is a verb that means "to sharpen." So taken literally, we are to sharpen our children. These are commands to us to be assertive in involving ourselves in the spiritual development of our children.[5]

The main instruction to fathers in the New Testament is similar. Paul states that the father's responsibilities to his children are to "bring them up in the training and admonition of the Lord" (Eph. 6:4). "Training" comes from the Greek verb "to educate"; the real meaning is a broad range of methods leading to a child's good upbringing. The methods include nurturing, chastening, and correcting, all summed up in discipline. "Admonition" refers to an education based on principles, the building of principles into a person's character.

Thus, a father's responsibilities are his children's training for discipline and instruction in principles. This is character building of the first order.

The key is to begin early. Younger children are very open to spiritual matters. Ask them who God is or what God is like. Such a question shows that you consider God a valid topic of conversation, and it gets them thinking. Clearly, you should not judge their response.

> **You could say, "The most important thing to know is that God is love and that He loves you and me and that His love will never stop."**

As I reflect on that, it is actually a great introduction to God for children of any age—the assurance that a heavenly Father loves them and cares for them at all times.

Will such teaching work? Solomon, reputed to be one of the wisest men who ever lived, provides a reassuring answer:

> My son, keep your father's command,
> And do not forsake the law of your mother.
> Bind them continually upon your heart;
> Tie them around your neck.
> When you roam, they will lead you;
> When you sleep, they will keep you;
> And when you awake, they will speak with you.
> For the commandment is a lamp,
> And the law a light;
> Reproofs of instruction are the way of life
> (Prov. 6:20-23).

That promise is exciting to us as fathers: we teach, and we are promised that our children will be guided when they walk, protected when they sleep, and encouraged when they awake.

The second half of the system laid out in Deuteronomy was talk: "Talk of them when you sit in your house, when you walk by the way, when you lie down, and when you rise up." Sitting, walking, lying down, and rising. In short, live the commandment. Model the love of God. I like Gordon MacDonald's characterization of it as "saturation leadership" involving three elements: (1) love God, (2) keep this love a high profile priority in your life, and (3) bathe every moment of your relationship with your kids in this reality.

I can't stress enough that men of faith must model their faith before their kids if their teaching and talking are going to do any good. Why?

For young children (up to around age five), you are the image of God to them. What they understand about God and how they feel about God will heavily depend on what they experience with you as a father. That is an awesome responsibility to bear. For your young children, "God has agreed to live with whatever image you project of who He is." [6]

Eight-year-old Zac Hansel presents this truth through a child's eyes:

> **After Zac said, "Amen," he lifted his head quietly. He looked around at all of us and then looked squarely at Joshua.**
>
> **"Josh, we can know what Jesus looks like."**
>
> **"How, Zac?" his little brother asked with great excitement.**
>
> **"That's why God made families, Josh,"** answered Zac simply.[7]

As kids get older, they are going to need more from you in modeling your faith. They are going to be asking, Is God real? Does He really care about me? Can He help me in my problems and crises? And they will be looking at how these are answered in Dad's life. So you need to show how God is at work in your life, and you need to tell them on occasion how God is working in your life. You also must be very aware that teens are quickly disillusioned by hypocrisy: they feel that if faith is to be real, it must be lived out with consistency between what is taught and done. They must see that your faith does not take a holiday.

You need to have in your family lots of "spiritual moments." No, they are not necessarily times of prayer or family devotions—which you certainly need. Rather, they are the moments when after a burst of anger and some ill-thought words, you say to your child or wife, "I'm sorry. That was wrong. Please forgive me." Teens, younger children, and adults are bound to "see God" in such spiritual moments.

Does modeling faith work in the lives of children? Here is one child, guitarist Dan Huff, who testifies how it did in his life:

> My parents were very serious about their faith, and they tried to make it relevant to our young lives. It took time, it took discussing, but through it all we grew to understand that faith in God is not just something you capsulize into a Sunday or an event—it's a way of life. I can see in my brothers and they can see in me (it's harder to see it in yourself) a real sense of compassion and a love for people that had to come from our parents. That's how they were and are, and only through a lot of time spent talking about our faith and seeing their example did we ever get to this point. I think I learned more about a godly life

> from those family discussions than I did from any
> teaching I ever received in church. I saw my folks
> live out their faith.[8]

Time now for part two of this section—how the dad who's not quite sure what he believes can introduce his child to God. Though it sounds like a contradiction in terms, it really is appropriate and not that difficult to do, according to Benjamin Spock. I cite him at some length because he makes many useful points and suggestions in *Dr. Spock on Parenting:*

> Talking with children about religion has been made more difficult in the past hundred years by the changing religious attitudes and weakening beliefs of many people. But the concept of the universe as a purely physical system and of the human being as merely a contraption made up of cells and chemicals, developed through the process of evolution, leaves many of us who are agnostics or are only vaguely religious feeling unsatisfied. We crave more meaning for our existence. We strongly sense a spiritual force within us and in those around us. We want to give that force a name and identity and to define our personal relationship with it....
>
> I think that questions such as, "Can I see God?" or, "Why can't I see God?" from a child at three, four, or five are hard to answer, even for church-going parents, because a spirit is intangible. They can help the child to see that it's not just his problem by saying, "Nobody can see God." Then parents can try to define a spirit by giving an example. "God is a spirit. That means God doesn't have a body like you or me. We believe God is every-

where, watching over us, listening to our prayers, loving us. You can't see the wind, can you? But you can feel it and you know it is there."

Nonbelieving parents can give the same kind of explanation, but instead of making it their own explanation, they can preface it by saying, "People who believe in God believe that God doesn't have a body like you or me. God is a spirit. That means God is everywhere," and so forth.

And if a child asks, "Do you believe in God?" I think that parents can say, "We do, but we don't know just what God is like." Or, "We don't, but we have a lot of friends who do. We believe in some of the things that Jesus taught." Or, "We don't. But when you are older, you may decide to believe in God."...

Vague believers and nonchurchgoing parents may answer questions about God and the Bible and heaven along the following lines: "The Bible is a book that was written thousands of years ago. It tells how a person named God made the whole world in the beginning. It says he made the sun and the moon and the stars, and the mountains and the oceans. It says he made all the animals and birds and fishes, and finally he made the people. Lots of people go to church on Sundays to sing songs to God and to thank him for all the good things they have, like delicious food and a nice house and warm clothes. These people also go to church to ask God to help them be good. The Bible says God lives in heaven, but we don't know where that is. Some say it is in the sky. People who go to church can't really see God there. But they feel he is there just the same, not as a body, but as a spirit."...

All but the most materialistic among us hold to strong spiritual values and beliefs, even if we never speak of them, and our children absorb them gradually and silently by living with us. But to hear them spoken of and to discuss them with us helps children to clarify spiritual beliefs and values, to select those aspects that have the most meaning and to adopt them as their own.[9]

From Dr. Spock on Parenting. Copyright © 1988 by Dr. Benjamin Spock. Reprinted by permission of Simon & Schuster, Inc.

INTRODUCING YOUR CHILDREN TO PRAYER

The following story is significant for you to hear as you consider the issue of introducing your children to prayer. It is the story of Ruby Bridges, a six-year-old African-American child in New Orleans in the days when schools in the South were first being desegregated. For months, Ruby had to walk past heckling mobs to and from school; people constantly hurled insults, jeered, and even spat at her.

How would you have responded in the situation? First, there is the incredible perseverance factor. I would have been sorely tempted to give up and stay away from so much trouble. But far more incredible are Ruby's response and attitude to the hecklers and spitters. Here is how a teacher described what she saw as she watched Ruby through the window walking to school one day:

The crowd was there, and shouting, as usual. A woman spat at Ruby but missed. Ruby smiled at her. A man shook his fist at her; Ruby smiled at him. Then she walked up the stairs and she stopped and turned and smiled one more time! You know what she told one of the marshals? She told him she prays for those people, the ones in that mob, every night before she goes to sleep.[10]

Ruby later told a psychoanalyst called in to advise the teachers:

> They keep coming and saying the bad words, but my momma says they'll get tired after a while and they'll stop coming. They'll stay home…. The minister says if I forgive the people and smile at them and pray for them, God will keep a good eye on everything, and He'll be our protection. I'm sure God knows what's happening, and He can't help but notice. He may not rush to do anything, not right away. But there will come a day, like you hear in church.[11]

That is why one often hears of the power of prayer. I can think of no other power that could have brought Ruby through those months with the attitude she had. And that's the kind of power that I want each of my children to have.

There are only two other points to be made about prayer. One is that probably nothing is more important that a dad can do for his children than to pray for them. In the book *Back to the Family* profiling one hundred successful families, the author concluded that a fundamental maxim in raising kids is to pray for them.

That is especially true for teens, who are much more out of our hands and control than younger children are. When I think of prayer and teenagers, I think of the example set by Joe White in regard to his own children:

> With a new teenager I realized all over again how the job of parenting was a lot bigger than my

abilities. That means a lot of prayer.

The Lord says, "You have not because you ask not," and "Ask, and you will receive, that your joy may be full." I figure that if one prayer is good, a thousand would be great. In this critical matter of raising teenagers, I want to get as close as possible to Paul's directive to "Pray without ceasing."

We can expect to have Jamie at home for only six teenage years. So for six years, I will concentrate in prayer for her... asking God to make them six golden years.

We ask with faith. God can do it. As Romans 8:32 suggests, if God thought enough of us to give us His Son, won't He also give us all things— including the wisdom and strength and love to help her make the most of this season in her life.

So we pray. We pray for all the people in her life: her friends, her teammates, her teachers and coaches, her future husband. We pray for her ability to withstand peer pressure. We pray for her self-image. We pray for her desire to honor and obey us. We pray for our wisdom guiding her. And I pray that the example of my life will be more consistently godly.[12]

The other point is to pray with your children. Our times of family prayer have brought me great joy in my fathering. Each Sunday night for the past year, we have closed our "share and prayer" family time with a five- to ten-minute time of conversational prayer. Nothing formal, artificial, or strange. Just a natural talking to God about the people and situations we have been discussing. I can honestly say that my major thrills as a dad have come (1) while hearing each of my children pray not only for

Mom and Dad, other family members, and world events but also for each other and (2) when we as a family have seen answers to our specific prayers.

It is an old adage, but I believe it is absolutely true: the family that prays together stays together.

ROOTEDNESS IN AN AGE OF INSTABILITY AND INSECURITY

This chapter has discussed instilling spiritual values in children. I have suggested that may be done through focusing on two areas: introducing them to God and introducing them to prayer.

Earlier, I highlighted some of the major benefits for your children by helping them to answer life's big questions, develop firm values to identify with, become more secure in their identity, and gain the confidence to face a sometimes hostile world.

I see these four benefits being summed up in the phrase "spiritual rootedness." By working to instill spiritual values in our children, we are working to give them a spiritual rootedness in this age of rapid change and insecurity. This spiritual rootedness gives them an inner settledness in their hearts and their souls, which comes from knowing that God is in control.

I was thrilled to see that my daughter Krista sensed this spiritual rootedness in her life at the tender age of ten when she wrote,

> **Dad couldn't be his loving, patient self without God's never-ending love and forgiveness in his heart and mind. Having quiet times and talking with God, reading the Bible and praying have all made my childhood, including now, less troublesome and more comforting.... I also thank Dad for making it part of our daily and weekly schedule to pray before eating, and to have family**

nights where we all get together and read and learn more about the Bible and where we pray for each other and others who need our prayers.

In the Bible, this idea of spiritual rootedness is graphically portrayed: "This hope we have as an anchor of the soul, both sure and steadfast." An "anchor of the soul." What a beautiful gift for children!

POINTS TO REMEMBER
- "Great fathers are they who see that for their children spiritual forces are stronger than material forces."
- So you must take stock and ask, What am I doing and what am I committed to regarding my children's spiritual development? Have I helped them in answering life's BIG questions: Who am I? What am I here for? What's the meaning of life?
- "One theme to emerge most prominently is spirituality, or the belief in a Creator and living by His guidelines. Nearly ninety percent of the families pointed to spirituality as a significant, if not dominant, guiding force in their lives."
- "The Lord, I think, is who holds this family together."
- As a dad, you can give your children many things but a relationship with God is not one of them.
- For a dad who has a strong belief in God, your first and foremost responsibility is to teach your children about God and to live a life consonant with your religious convictions.
- A father's responsibilities are his children's training for discipline and instruction in principles. This is character building of the first order.
- This promise is exciting to us as fathers: we teach, and we are promised that our children will be guided when they walk, protected when they sleep, and encouraged when they awake.
- Men of faith must model their faith before their kids if their

teaching and talking are going to do any good.

- You need to have in your family lots of "spiritual moments"—moments when after a burst of anger and some ill-thought words, you say to your child or wife, "I'm sorry. That was wrong. Please forgive me."
- "She told him she prays for those people, the ones in that mob, every night before she goes to sleep."
- Probably nothing is more important that a dad can do for his children than to pray for them.
- "We can expect to have Jamie at home for only six teenage years. So for six years, I will concentrate in prayer for her… asking God to make them six golden years."
- Pray with your children. Our times of family prayer have brought me joy in my fathering.
- "Having quiet times and talking with God, reading the Bible and praying have all made my childhood, including now, less troublesome and more comforting."
- An "anchor of the soul." What a beautiful gift for children!

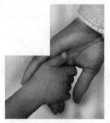

CONCLUSION

Refined to its most basic elements, successful parenting is unconditional love, commitment, training by example, and the willingness to discipline.
—DR. RAY GUARENDI

I TRUST that you have sensed that this book has not been based so much on head knowledge as on heart knowledge. I am a man with a passion for fathering, and I want this passion to burn in the hearts of as many dads as possible.

I hope that as we come to the end of this book, you will be as excited as I am to view the days and months ahead as the beginning of an adventure in the joy of fathering. You should know that as I was writing this book, I, too, was learning along with you.

KEY CHARACTERISTICS OF A STRONG FAMILY

These words about what a home is move me deeply:

> Whatever else may be said about the home, it is the bottom line of life, the anvil upon which attitudes and convictions are hammered out. It is the place where life's bills come due, the single most influential force in our earthly existence. No price tag can adequately reflect its value. No gauge can measure its ultimate influence... for good or ill. It is at home, among family members, that we come

to terms with circumstances. IT IS HERE LIFE MAKES UP ITS MIND.[1]

Thinking of the values being communicated today by pop culture, I'm glad that the home is where "LIFE MAKES UP ITS MIND." It is here that I want my children to build their character and form their basic moral and spiritual values.

As we seek to establish and build a good home life, we can learn from the results of some studies that have sought to define the essential elements of a strong family. One list came from a summary review of research studies conducted over recent decades.[2] A second list came from a recent study of three thousand strong families in South America, Switzerland, Austria, Germany, South Africa, and the United States.[3] A third list came from interviews by Jeane Westin, who authored *The Coming Parent Revolution.*[4] One strong family element was cited in all three lists while five other elements were cited in two of three lists. Here, then, are the six key characteristics of a strong family:

1. The family has a spiritual commitment (all three lists).
2. Members love each other, and the family is a unit.
3. Family members spend time together.
4. Good communication between family members exists.
5. Ability to solve problems in a crisis is common.
6. Family members express appreciation to each other.

You can't go wrong if you strive for these elements in your family.

THREE FINAL FATHERING TIPS
As we set out on this adventure to establish a strong family and in the process experience the real joy of fathering, I would like to leave three final fathering tips with you.

My first tip is to be enthusiastic about your fathering, always remembering that you cannot fail as a dad until you completely quit trying to be a great dad. Flee from such expressions as "I don't care" or "I give up," for when they are heard too often the ball game is over. Embrace the fact that you can't fail because there is no "right" way to raise a child. Rather, there are many right ways, so keep experimenting and find those that work best for you and your kids. John Powell, in a discussion of how the average person accomplishes only 10 percent of his promise and his heart is only 10 percent alive with love, closes with these powerful words: "He will die without ever having really lived or really loved. To me, this is the most frightening of all possibilities. I would really hate to think that you or I might die without having really lived and really loved."[5]

Dad, be alive to your family. Really live! And really love your children!

Keep on trying up to your final breath. As you think about your lifelong commitment to your children, remember the never-quit attitude embodied in these words:

> Daddy is the one who finds the way to tell his children, no matter what they do, no matter where they go, no matter how long it's been, no matter how old they are, no matter what it costs—
> If I have a penny, you'll never be broke.
> If I have a pork chop, you won't go hungry.
> If I have a shirt, you won't be cold.
> If I have an arm, you'll always be hugged.
> And if I don't have a penny, or a pork chop, or a shirt, or enough power in my tired arms to hug anymore, come stand by my bed and hold my hand,

and know that if there's a heart left in this old body, then Daddy still loves you.[6]

My second fathering tip is to find someone to hold you accountable. Many times, dads hear a talk or read something, and they get all excited about putting it into practice. But then they find they can't stick to it. This is where a good friend comes in— confide your goals and ask for accountability. I have been privileged to have such a friend, John Bernbaum, for the past fifteen years. His advice and counsel, just plain listening, and constant support and encouragement have been invaluable to me in my spiritual journey and in my role as husband and father.

The third tip is a word of encouragement. As you look forward to investing time in your family's well-being, you will get back what you put in. By all accounts, your investment of time in your children will help bring about in them a healthy self-concept, higher self-esteem, higher self-confidence in personal and social interaction, greater moral maturity, reduced risks of unwed teen pregnancy, greater internal control, and higher career aspirations.

What do you have on this earth that is most valuable to you? The members of your family. You must never lose this perspective on where you should invest much of your time and energies. To help burn it into your mind, I want to close with a personal story told by J. Allan Petersen about the true values of family relationships:

> Every nook and cranny of the big 747 was crowded. It took off in the middle of the night in Brazil where I'd been speaking. As it moved into the night I began to doze. I don't know how long I slept, but I was starting to wake when I heard a strong voice announcing, "We have a very serious

emergency." Three engines had gone because of fuel contamination, and the other engine would go any second.

The steward said in English, "Now you must do exactly as we tell you. Don't anyone think of doing anything we do not suggest. Your life depends on us. We are trained for your safety, so you must do exactly as we tell you."

Then he rattles this off in Portuguese. Everybody looked soberly at one another.

The steward said, "Now pull down the curtains, in a few minutes we are going to turn off all the lights."

My thought exclaimed, "Lord."

The plane veered and banked, as the crew tried to get it back to the airport. The steward ran up and down the aisle and barked out orders, "Now take that card out of the seat pocket, and I want you to look at this diagram." You know, I've flown millions of miles over the world and here I thought I had the card memorized, but I panicked because I couldn't find the crazy card. Everybody looked stunned as we felt the plane plunge down.

Finally, the steward said, "Now tighten the seat belts as tight as you can, and pull up your legs and bury your head in your lap." We couldn't look out to see where we were—high or low.

I peeked around—the Portuguese were crossing themselves, and I thought, "This is it. This is serious. I can't believe this. I didn't know this was going to happen tonight. I guess this is it." And I had a crazy sensation.

Then the steward's voice broke into my

consciousness, barking out in this machine-gun fashion, "Prepare for impact." Frankly, I wasn't thinking about the photocopier. I wasn't worried about the oil in my car. At times like that, involuntarily, from deep inside of us, something comes out that's never structured, planned, or rehearsed. And all I could do was pray. Everybody started to pray. I found myself praying in a way I never thought of doing. As I buried my head in my lap and pulled my knees up, as I was convinced it was over I said, "Oh, God, thank You. Thank You for the incredible privilege of knowing You. Life has been wonderful." And as the plane was going down my last thought, my last cry, "Oh, God, my wife! My children!"

Now I should say for the sake of you, the reader, that I survived! As I wandered about in the middle of the night in the airport with a knot in my stomach and cotton in my mouth, I couldn't speak. I ached all over.

I thought, "What did I do? What did I say? What were my last thoughts? Why did I think that?" I wondered, "What was the bottom line?"

Here's the bottom line: relationship.

When I... saw my wife at the airport, I looked at her and rushed to hold her hand. I just looked at her a moment then threw my arms around her and said, "Oh, I appreciate you." And then with tears in my eyes, I looked at her again, and sold, "I appreciate you so much. I didn't even know if I'd ever see you again; oh, I appreciate you."

When I arrived home, I found my three sons and said, "I appreciate you. Boy, I'm glad you're in this house and I'm part of you."

I am only one, you are only one. But because we are in a family we hold a piece of the puzzle in our own power. And what we can do, we should do. I trust that you will say with me, "And by the grace of God, I will do what I can do in my home."[7]

NOTES

Introduction: Experience the Joy

1. Joe White, *Orphans at Home* (Phoenix: Questar, 1988), p. 134.
2. Tony and Bart Campolo, *Things We Wish We Had Said* (Dallas: Word, 1989), p. 213.

Your Fathering Legacy

1. Steve Farrar, *Point Man* (Portland, Oreg.: Multnomah, 1990), p.48.
2. Chuck Swindoll, *The Strong Family* (Portland, Oreg.: Multnomah, 1991), p. 76.
3. Cited in Charles Williams, *Forever a Father, Always a Son* (Wheaton: Victor, 1991), p. 142.
4. Josh McDowell and Dick Day, *How to Be a Hero to Your Kids* (Dallas: Word, 1991), pp. 113–14. Used by permission.
5. Ibid., p. 149.
6. Paul Lewis, *Famous Fathers* (Elgin: David C. Cook, 1984), p. 25.
7. Cited in Williams, p. 21.

Chapter 1

1. James C. Dobson, *Parenting Isn't for Cowards* (Dallas: Word, 1987), pp. 186–88. Used by permission.
2. Erma Bombeck, *Family—The Ties that Bind... and Gag!* (New York: Fawcett, 1988), p. 2.
3. Samuel Osherson, *Finding Our Fathers* (New York: Fawcett/Columbine, 1986), p. 6.
4. Ibid., p. 7.
5. Ibid., p. 54.
6. Josh McDowell and Dick Day, *How to Be a Hero to Your Kids* (Dallas: Word, 1991), p. 223. Used by permission.
7. Ray Guarendi, *Back to the Family* (New York: Villard, 1990), p. 118.
8. Tony and Bart Campolo, *Things We Wish We Had Said* (Dallas: Word,

1989), p. 33.

9. Marianne Neifert, *Dr. Mom's Parenting Guide* (New York: Dutton, 1991), p. 28.

10. Gordon MacDonald, *The Effective Father* (Wheaton: Tyndale, 1977), p. 79.

11. Guarendi, pp. 125–26.

Chapter 2

1. Virginia Hearn, ed., *What They Did Right* (Wheaton: Tyndale, 1974), p. 131.

2. Stephen A. Bly, *How to Be a Good Dad* (Chicago: Moody, 1986), p. 61.

3. Kay Kuzma, *Prime Time Parenting* (New York: Rawson, Wade, 1980), p. 21.

4. Ibid., p.158.

5. Gloria Gaither, ed., *What My Parents Did Right* (Nashville: Star Song, 1991), pp. 78–79.

6. Bruce Larson, *The One and Only You* (Waco: Word, 1974).

Chapter 4

1. Told in *Tools for Time Management* by Edward R. Dayton (Grand Rapids: Zondervan, 1974), pp. 64–65.

2. Albert Siegel, Stanford Observer, as quoted in *The Wittenburg Door* (San Diego: Youth Specialties).

3. Kyle Pruett, *The Nurturing Father* (New York: Warner, 1987).

4. Ibid., pp. 17–18.

Chapter 5

1. James C. Dobson, *Parenting Isn't for Cowards* (Dallas: Word, 1987), pp. 142–43. Used by permission.

2. Ross Campbell, *How to Really Love Your Teenager* (Wheaton: Victor, 1981), p. 77.

3. Ibid., p. 29.

4. Judith Allen Shelly, *The Spiritual Needs of Children* (Downers Grove,

Ill.: InterVarsity, 1982), p. 72.

5. Josh McDowell and Dick Day, *Why Wait?* (San Bernardino: Here's Life, 1987), p. 65.

6. Ibid., p. 64.

7. Merton P. Strommen and Irene A. Strommen, *Five Cries of Parents* (San Francisco: Harper & Row, 1985), p. 72.

8. Campbell, p. 77.

9. Lawrence Bauman with Robert Riche, *The Nine Most Troublesome Teenage Problems* (Secaucus, N.J.: Lyle Stuart, 1986), p. 27.

10. Joseph R. Novello, *Bringing Up Kids American Style* (New York: A & W Publishers, 1981), p. 4.

11. Josh McDowell, *What I Wish My Parents Knew about My Sexuality* (San Bernardino: Here's Life, 1987), pp. 54–55.

12. Abigail Wood, "The Trouble with Dad," *Seventeen*, October 1985, p. 38.

Chapter 6

1. Theodore Roosevelt in an address before the First International Congress in America on the Welfare of the Child, March 1908.

2. Robert Bly as interviewed in "A Gathering of Men" (New York: Public Affairs Television, 1990), p. 13.

3. Joseph Novello, *Bringing Up Kids American Style* (New York: A & W Publishers, 1981), pp.136–37.

4. Quoted in Charles Williams, *Forever a Father, Always a Son* (Wheaton: Victor, 1991), p. 87.

Chapter 7

1. Cited in Joe White, *Orphans at Home* (Phoenix: Questar, 1988), pp. 161–63.

2. Paul Lewis, *Famous Fathers* (Elgin: David C. Cook, 1984), p. 131.

3. Ross Campbell, *How to Really Love Your Teenager* (Wheaton: Victor, 1981), pp. 13–15.

4. White, p. 102.

5. Tony and Bart Campolo, *Things We Wish We Had Said* (Dallas: Word, 1989), p. 191.

6. Jim Sanderson, *How to Raise Your Kids to Stand on Their Own Two Feet* (New York: Congdon & Weed, 1978), p. 36.

7. Ibid., pp. 41–42.

8. Josh McDowell and Dick Day, *How to Be a Hero to Your Kids* (Dallas: Word, 1990), p. 135. Used by permission.

9. Phil McCombs, "Men's Movement Stalks the Wild Side," *Washington Post*, February 3, 1991, pp. F1 and F6.

10. Robert E. Fisher, *Quick to Listen, Slow to Speak* (Wheaton: Tyndale, 1987), p. 40.

11. Ray Guarendi, *Back to the Family* (New York: Villard, 1990), p. 149.

12. Sanderson, p. 40.

13. Rolf Garborg, *The Family Blessing* (Dallas: Word, 1990), pp. 45–47.

14. Gary Smalley and John Trent, *The Blessing* (New York: Pocket Books, 1979), p. 47.

15. Ibid., pp. 223–29.

16. Gloria Gaither, ed., *What My Parents Did Right* (Nashville: Star Song, 1991), pp. 115–16.

Chapter 8

1. Debora Phillips, *How to Give Your Child a Great Self-Image* (New York: Random House, 1989), p. 7.

2. Louise Hart, *The Winning Family* (New York: Dodd, Mead, 1987), p. 5.

3. Joe White, *Orphans at Home* (Phoenix: Questar, 1988), p. 129.

4. Hart, p. 11.

5. James Dobson, *Hide or Seek* (Old Tappan, N.J.: Revell, 1974), pp. 20–21.

6. Tony and Bart Campolo, *Things We Wish We Had Said* (Dallas: Word, 1989), p. 141.

7. Dobson, p. 19.

8. Dobson, pp. 23–24.

9. Ibid., p. 43.

10. Josh McDowell and Norm Wakefield, *The Dad Difference* (San Bernardino: Here's Life, 1989), p. 13.

11. Paul Lewis, *Famous Fathers* (Elgin: David C. Cook, 1984), p. 111.

12. Christopher Andersen, *Father: The Figure and the Force* (New York: Warner Books, 1983), p. 75.

13. Elyce Wakerman, *Father Loss* (Garden City, N.Y.: Doubleday, 1984), pp. 272–73.

14. Spencer Johnson, *The One Minute Father* (New York: William Morrow, 1983), p. 69.

15. White, pp. 144–45.

16. Results of study cited in Dobson, p. 92.

17. Steve Farrar, *Point Man* (Portland, Oreg.: Multnomah, 1990), pp. 219–20.

18. Zig Ziglar, *Raising Positive Kids in a Negative World* (New York: Ballantine Books, 1985), p.176.

19. Ibid., p. 52.

20. White, p. 23.

21. Johnson, pp. 79–80.

22 Campolo, p. 145.

23 James Harris, *You and Your Child's Self-Esteem* (New York: Carroll & Graf, 1989), p.125.

Chapter 9

1. H. Stephen Glenn and Jane Nelsen, *Raising Self-Reliant Children in a Self-Indulgent World* (Rocklin, Calif.: Prima Publishing and Communications, 1988), p. 208.

2. Ibid.

3. Virginia Hearn, ed., *What They Did Right* (Wheaton: Tyndale, 1974), p. 240.

4. Charles Williams, *Forever a Father, Always a Son* (Wheaton: Victor, 1991), pp. 168–69.

5. Tim Hansel, *What Kids Need Most in a Dad* (Tarrytown, N.Y.: Revell, 1984), p. 167.

6. Ray Guarendi, *Back to the Family* (New York: Villard, 1990), p.135.

7. Hearn, pp. 68–69.

8. Hansel, p. 74.

9. Joe White, *Orphans at Home* (Phoenix: Questar, 1988), p. 87

10. Josh McDowell and Norm Wakefield, *The Dad Difference* (San Bernardino: Here's Life, 1989), p. 56.

Chapter 10

1. E. Kent Hayes, *Why Good Parents Have Bad Kids* (New York: Doubleday, 1989), p. 51.

2. Bruno Bettelheim, *A Good Enough Parent* (New York: Knopf, 1987), p. 99.

3. Cited in Paul Lewis, *Famous Fathers* (Elgin: David C. Cook, 1984), p. 65.

4. Tim Hansel, *What Kids Need Most in a Dad* (Tarrytown, N.Y.: Revell, 1984), p. 140.

5. Bruce Narramore, *Adolescence Is Not an Illness* (Old Tappan, N.J.: Revell, 1980), pp. 67–68.

6. Adapted from David Augsburger, *Caring Enough to Confront* (Glendale, Calif.: Regal Books, 1980), pp. 13–15.

7. Cited in Gordon MacDonald, *The Effective Father* (Wheaton: Tyndale, 1977), pp. 125–26.

8. Hayes, pp. 104–5.

9. Virginia Hearn, ed., *What They Did Right* (Wheaton: Tyndale, 1974), p. 55.

Chapter 11

1. Neil Kurshan, *Raising Your Child to Be a Mensch* (New York: Atheneum, 1987), p. 11.

2. Joseph Novello, *Bringing Up Kids American Style* (New York: A & W Publishers, 1981), p. 5.

3. Jeane Westin, *The Coming Parent Revolution* (Chicago: Rand McNally, 1981), p. 205.

4. Ibid., p. 206.

5. Novello, p. 7.

6. Virginia Hearn, ed., *What They Did Right* (Wheaton: Tyndale, 1974), p. 240.

7. Tony and Bart Campolo, *Things We Wish We Had Said* (Dallas: Word, 1989), p. 40.

8. Kurshan, pp. 12–13.

9. Donald M. Joy, *Parents, Kids, and Sexual Integrity* (Waco: Word, 1988), p. 16.

10. Gloria Gaither, ed., *What My Parents Did Right* (Nashville: Star Song, 1991), p. 48.

11. Rolf Zettersten, "Giving Our Children the Gift of Compassion," *Focus on the Family*, July 1991, p. 14.

12. James M. Harris, *You and Your Child's Self-Esteem* (New York: Carroll & Graf, 1989), pp. 53–54.

Chapter 12

1. *Saint Augustine's Confessions*, trans. with an introduction by R. S. Pine-Coffin (Harmondsworth, Middlesex, England: Penguin, 1961), p. 45.

2. Ray Guarendi, *Back to the Family* (New York: Villard, 1990), p. 102.

3. Benjamin Spock, *Dr. Spock on Parenting* (New York: Simon and Schuster, 1988), p. 22.

4. Guarendi, p. 105.

5. These points are found in Chuck Swindoll, *The Strong Family* (Portland, Oreg.: Multnomah, 1991), p. 19.

6. Donald M. Joy, *Parents, Kids, and Sexual Integrity* (Waco: Word, 1988), p. 177.

7. Tim Hansel, *What Kids Need Most in a Dad* (Tarrytown, N.Y.: Revell, 1984), p. 37.

8. Gloria Gaither, ed., *What My Parents Did Right* (Nashville: Star Song, 1991), p. 115.

9. Spock, pp. 262, 266-67, 269.

10. Sheila Kitzinger and Celia Kitzinger, *Tough Questions* (Boston: Harvard

Common Press, 1991), p. 204.

11. Ibid., p. 205.

12. Joe White, *Orphans at Home* (Phoenix: Questar, 1988), pp. 223–24.

Conclusion

1. Charles R. Swindoll, *Home: Where Life Makes Up Its Mind* (Portland, Oreg.: Multnomah, 1979), p. 5.

2. An unpublished summary review by Dr. Judson Swihart (at the Department of Human Development and Family Studies, Kansas State University).

3. Nick Stinnett, "Six Qualities that Make Families Strong," chapter 1 in *Family Building: Six Qualities of a Strong Family*, ed. George Rekers (Ventura, Calif.: Regal Books, 1985), p. 38.

4. Jeane Westin, *The Coming Parent Revolution* (Chicago: Rand McNally, 1981), pp. 256–58.

5. John Powell, *The Secret of Staying in Love* (Allen, Texas: Argus Communications, 1974), p. 11.

6. Stephen A. Bly, *How to Be a Good Dad* (Chicago: Moody, 1986), p. 129.

7. J. Allan Petersen, "Expressing Appreciation," chapter 4 in *Rekers*, pp. 103–6. Used by permission.

ABOUT THE AUTHOR

Dr. Robert Hamrin is the founder and president of Great Dads, an international ministry whose vision is to help turn the hearts of fathers to their children. He is also becoming well known as Dr. Bob, his "title" at the Great Dads Gathering Place, a comprehensive fathering resource center at www.greatdads.org.

Bob's fathering emphasis began with the deep joy and fulfillment he found in being a father to his three children. He has appeared as a guest on over 40 television and radio talk shows on fathering.

Prior to founding Great Dads, he served (1983–1996) as an independent economic-business consultant, author, and speaker. In his government days from 1974 to 1983, he served as a staff economist for the Joint Economic Committee of Congress, the EPA, a Presidential Commission, and a U.S. Senator.

He and his wife, Carol, live in the country town of Clifton, Virginia, outside of Washington, D.C. They have three grown children: Eric, Krista, and Kira.

YOU CAN HELP FATHERS BECOME GREAT DADS BY

HELPING TO HOST A SEMINAR
and/or
BECOMING AN ASSOCIATE

You can help fathers become Great Dads—simply by encouraging your church, company, or other organization to host a Great Dads seminar.

These seminars, held across America and Europe, have already trained over 5,500 dads in The 6 Basics of Being a Great Dad. All the dads, and the seminar host organizations, have received it enthusiastically, with many of the dads saying how it transformed their life and their relationships with their children.

Also, if you have a heart for fathering and would like to train dads by being a seminar leader, get in touch with Bob Hamrin. Great Dads is always looking for a "few good men" to add to its Associates team. It's easy to be an Associate as the commitment is simply to initiate one seminar a year.

For further information on helping to host a seminar or to become an Associate, please contact Great Dads at:

1-888-GRTDADS
Grtdads@aol.com

Please visit our comprehensive fathering resource center
Great Dads Gathering Place at
www.greatdads.org